YOU AND YOUR BOAT
by
George Lesko

Illustrated by G. diPalma and J. M. Sedacca

Do you like to water ski? Skin-dive? Fish? Race? All of these pleasures are possible with a boat, the right boat, given correct care. Boating used to be an important method of transportation and now is an everyday luxury, depending upon your pocketbook and where you live. Here are suggestions for *what to buy*, the different kinds of boats and their care, precautions you should take, the rules of safety dealing with seamanship and navigation, and equipment needed. Half the fun of owning a boat is the caring for it, so included in this book are directions for a job well done, plus diagrams for mooring instructions on through artificial respiration — you might need all of them. Enjoy your boat!

* * * * * *

Classification and Dewey Decimal: Boats (797.1)

About the Author:

A native of McKeesport, Pennsylvania, GEORGE LESKO now lives in Pittsburgh with his family. He has contributed articles to various magazines and was Associate Editor of *Popular Boating* for several years. This is his first book.

GEORGE LESKO

YOU AND YOUR
BOAT

Illustrated by G. diPalma
and J.M. Sedacca

1967 FIRST CADMUS EDITION
THIS SPECIAL EDITION IS PUBLISHED BY ARRANGEMENT WITH
THE PUBLISHERS OF THE REGULAR EDITION
LOTHROP, LEE & SHEPARD CO., INC.
BY
E. M. HALE AND COMPANY
EAU CLAIRE, WISCONSIN

© 1964 by George Lesko
Library of Congress Catalog Card Number: 64-14445
All rights reserved.
Designed by Patricia Ayearst

This edition lithographed in U. S. A. by Wetzel Bros., Inc., Milwaukee 2, Wisconsin

Contents

Chapter One

YOUR FIRST BOAT   13

Buying a Used Boat · Building *versus* Buying
· Hull Forms · Catamarans · Rubber and
Canvas Boats · Wooden Boats · Metal Boats ·
Fiberglass Boats · Types of Powerboats ·
Selecting an Engine · A Used Engine · Your
Test Ride · Financing Your Boat · Insure Your
Boat

Chapter Two

THE FIRST DAY WITH YOUR BOAT   51

The Controls · Starting Your Engine · Going
Aboard · Underway · Home Again · Mooring
Procedures

Chapter Three

SAFETY   81

Causes of Accidents · Safety Equipment ·
Numbering Your Boat · Fueling Safety ·
Flotation Material · Artificial Respiration ·
Courtesy Motorboat Examination · Organiza-
tions Dedicated to Safe Boating · Safety
Check · Courtesy—Key to Safety

Chapter Four

SEAMANSHIP 113

Rules of the Road • Navigation • Nautical
Charts • The Compass • River Cruising • Offshore Boating • Towing a Boat • Be Weather-
wise • Anchoring • Knots

Chapter Five

YOUR TRAILER 143

Matching Boat to Trailer • Trailer Hitches •
Maneuvering Your Trailer • Launching and
Retrieving • Trailer Accessories • Trailer Main-
tenance • Licensing Your Trailer • Before You
Set Out • Overland Cruising • Boating Season

Chapter Six

TAKING CARE OF YOUR BOAT 159

Topsides • Jobbing Out Work • Work You Can
Do • Painting Procedure • Painting Hints •
Minor Outboard Motor Work • Filling the
Gearbox • Trouble Shooting • In-Season Main-
tenance • Going Out of Commission • Where
to Store the Boat • Selecting a Boatyard • Your
Boat's Lay-up • Winterizing Your Gear •
Winterizing the Motor • Covering the Boat

Chapter Seven
ENJOYING YOUR BOAT   189
Swimming · Fishing · Water-Skiing · Skin
Diving · Photography · Underwater Photog-
raphy · Cruising · The Ship's Log · What to
Eat on a Cruise · What to Take on a Cruise ·
Cruising in Company · Games

Chapter Eight
TEST YOUR BOATING
KNOWLEDGE   237
Forty-three questions and answers based on
the suggested examination for seamanship-
course students of the Outboard Boating Club
of America.

GLOSSARY OF
NAUTICAL TERMS   243

SUGGESTED ADDITIONAL
READING   253

". . . There is *nothing*—absolutely nothing—half so much worth doing as simply messing about in boats."

—*The Wind in the Willows*

You and Your Boat

CHAPTER ONE

Your First Boat

Ever since primitive man first took to the water with a hollowed-out log for a craft in quest of food or to navigate a lake or stream, boating has exercised a magic spell over the human mind. Once a necessity for man's survival, it has become one of his favorite diversions. The application of motor power to boats greatly increased the scope of water travel, but for years it remained a sport for the rich. Now, with the development of powerful outboard engines and swift, sturdy hulls at low prices, it is within the reach of millions. You have seen highways thronged with cars carrying small boats slung over the top, trailers carrying runabouts, and trucks hauling cruisers to the nearest shore or riverbank, and perhaps you have succumbed to the lure of boating.

Owning a boat may seem complicated when you first

consider it. You may feel you lack the technical knowledge to buy, build, or maintain one. Getting the right boat, keeping it up, providing docking or storage, not to mention all the accessories you need, can run into time, effort, and money.

It's true that owning a boat is not so simple as owning a car; but actually it is not so difficult or complex as it may seem to the beginner. It can become relatively simple if you will undertake a careful study of boats and nagivation—a study which in itself is a pleasure. The means of acquiring all the knowledge you'll need to become a boat owner are close at hand.

In recent years, improvements in engines and hulls, and competition among many manufacturers, have made a wide choice of boats available to the prospective boatman—a choice so wide that he can hardly make a prudent selection without surveying the whole field carefully.

The best way to begin is to ask yourself a few simple questions.

What kind of boat should you buy? Which of the many models and makes available is the right boat for you, the one that will give you the most pleasure at the least expense? Here you'll have to consider some factors which may not have occurred to you. First, who is going to use the boat, and for what purposes? If you were buying an automobile, the answer would be easy. But boats and waterways are not so simple and standardized as cars and highways. When you buy a car, you already know how many passengers it can carry and where it will be going. A four-door sedan can carry six passengers without affecting its stability, but if you put six people in a small runabout, the performance and safety of the craft are drastically altered. So think first of who will be using the boat and its general purpose. Is it for yourself and one guest, or for the family? How many passengers must it carry?

Next, what are you going to use the boat for? If it is for fishing only, you will need one of a specific design, power and equipment that will be safe, convenient, and economical for this purpose. If you want to do a good deal of cruising, you might think of a cabin cruiser or a runabout with a convertible top and side curtains. Or perhaps you want a boat for water skiing. Consider the demands you'll be making of your boat before you even begin to shop for it.

Where will you use the boat? Thanks to automobiles and trailers and highways, you may have a choice of boating on inland waterways, lakes, or on the ocean. Where you'll be using the boat will make a big difference in your choice. A smooth-flowing river or a sheltered bay might be ideal for a lightweight runabout, but take that same boat into rough offshore waters and you're in for trouble—it could break apart, swamp, or capsize in large waves. On the other hand, a sturdy-hulled boat that rides deep in the water and is designed for rough seas would be impractical on a quiet lake—it would go much too slowly and probably eat up too much gas.

How much can you spend for your boat? At any given sum you can afford, there is some range of choice. The important thing is to make sure you get what you pay for.

SHOPPING FOR A BOAT

Once you have made your decisions on how and where you want to use your boat and how much you can pay, you can begin to look around. Now is the time to avail yourself of the wealth of free information you can find in the boating columns of newspapers, boating magazines, books, and many other sources. Start building a boating library now. It will be invaluable to you not only in selecting a boat but in operating, maintaining, and enjoying it over the years.

From your reading you can become familiar with the names of boat manufacturers and the kind of craft they offer in your price range. Write to them for catalogues and brochures with complete information on their models and prices. Usually this will cost you no more than a five-cent stamp. Of course each manufacturer will extol the virtues of his own product, but by obtaining a number of brochures you will be able to make comparative judgments on the specific model and make that suits your needs.

Once you've narrowed your choice down to about three or four different boats, visit the dealer in your area who handles each model. If one of the boats you like is not represented by a dealer near you, take a trip down to the nearest boat dock and try to find the owner of a boat made by the company whose product you are interested in. If you are inexperienced, you can learn more about a boat from its owner than by reading about it or testing the craft yourself. The owner knows how the boat handles and performs under conditions very similar to those you will be encountering. Every comment he makes should be taken seriously. Of course, some of the things he may tell you about the boat will not pertain to the way you plan to use your boat. But getting a firsthand report from an owner is invaluable.

If there is no dealer or owner of the kind of boat you want in your area, you may have to bypass this means of selection. You can order a boat and have it delivered before actually trying it out. However, this is not the most satisfactory procedure, and you also miss a good deal of the pleasure that comes from choosing your own boat on the basis of your own judgment.

Boat shows are fun, and they are also useful in helping you make your selection. Almost every major manufacturer is represented; they have models on display and people at their booths to answer questions. Here again you can make comparisons and develop your judgment. Engine and accessories manufacturers are also represented at local boat shows, so you can gather data on everything that you will need at one central location. Almost every city of any size has a boat show some time during the year, usually between September and April. Check with your local Chamber of Commerce to find out when the next show will be held in your area, or write to the National Association of Engine and Boat Manufacturers, 420 Lexington Avenue, New York.

Your local marine dealers also can be relied on to give you helpful information on the kind of boat you want. They will, of course, try to sell you the kind of boat they handle, but by talking to several of them, you can get a good idea of what each boat offers. The dealer must stand behind the product he sells, and so you can count on excellent service—

an important factor once you own a boat. To find your local marine dealers, look in the classified section of the telephone book under "Boats—Motor" or "Marine."

The classified section of the newspaper is another place to look for boats for sale. Most of the boats listed there will be used, but there will be a number of new boats as well.

Time is an important factor when you're shopping for a boat. If you go out and buy the first boat in your price range as soon as the idea pops into your head, you are in for trouble and expense. Take your time shopping, and select the right time to buy. Probably the best season is fall or early winter—especially if you live where boating is a seasonal sport. Many people decide to sell their boats after the summer season, since winter storage can be expensive. And the new boat market is usually most heavily stocked in fall and early winter. Prices will be slightly lower—or at least the dealer will be more willing to give you the best deal possible.

BUYING A USED BOAT

It is more exciting and more satisfactory to buy a new boat; but a used boat can be just as seaworthy, just as good-looking, and just as much fun.

If you buy a used boat you will probably get more boat for your money. But you may also put so much into repairs and maintenance that you will end up paying as much or more than you would for a comparable new boat. Be sure to check out the seaworthiness of any used boat that is offered for sale. Minor repairs *can* be fun and purchasing a used boat *can* save you money—but don't buy blindly.

It's pretty difficult to hide defects in a used boat, since a boat that is not kept in good repair deteriorates rapidly. Check your boat from all angles before purchasing it. Don't buy a homemade boat of the one-of-a-kind variety. It may not even float. At best, it will probably prove to be sluggish or unseaworthy. Don't buy a boat that has been built and designed by an amateur. Professional designers spend many hundreds of hours studying the proper construction of boats before they set a line on paper. It's reasonable to expect that a boat should be properly designed for stress, strain, and seaworthiness. Stay clear of all home-designed jobs.

Beware of novelty boats. They may look clever and pretty in the water, but chances are that's all they are.

Be wary of deals. If the price is ridiculously low, there is probably something wrong.

Try to get an experienced boatman to help you select your boat. You can benefit from his knowledge.

If you have a boat already and want to purchase a new one, make sure you sell your old boat before buying the new. Most dealers won't accept a trade-in, and used boats often take a while to sell. If you don't get rid of the old before buying the new, you may find yourself the surprised and unwilling owner of a small fleet.

BUILDING *VERSUS* BUYING

If you cannot find the boat you want at your price, you might be tempted to build your own. In this case, your first consideration should be whether or not you would actually enjoy building it. If sawdust runs in your veins and you'd rather spend a Saturday afternoon puttering around a shop than at a ball game, then perhaps you might want to build. Otherwise forget it while you're still in love with boating, and save your money for a very special buy. Building a boat is a tedious and exacting task. If you don't like the work, you won't get the result you want—if you finish it at all.

But if you like to build things and have a talent with tools, then here are some practical matters to think of:

How much time do you have at your disposal to devote to the job? How soon do you want to be underway? You can't build a boat by working only Saturday afternoons and expect to have it done in a month. Time makes a difference as well in the kind of boat you decide to build. If you want a cruiser, you might have to devote all your free time for a whole summer. If you're anxious to get on the water, forget building and buy.

Next, where will you build your boat? You need a garage, a back yard, or other large area. If the weather is changeable, you will have to have a heated place to build your boat. It will have to have an even temperature at all times to prevent warping, cracking, and splitting, and to allow glue to dry evenly. And since you'll be working a long, long time, you will need comfortable working conditions. Be sure you have at least 4 feet of working area on all sides of the boat.

Be sure also that you will be able to move your boat out of the building area to the water without tearing down walls or fences. You remember the story about the man who built a boat in his living room, then couldn't get it out the door.

If your garage is part of your home, bear in mind that fiberglassing the hull of the boat will cause a disagreeable odor that will penetrate into your living quarters.

Wherever you build your boat, you will need power tools, and electric outlets for them. You must be able to handle power tools as easily as manual ones. You will have to put literally thousands of screws into place, and without a power screwdriver, you'll be seeing them in your sleep for years.

What type of boat will you build? This will probably settle the matter of whether you build or buy. A simple pram can be a delight to build, and there's really not too much that can go wrong. However, if your experience in carpentry is limited and you are pining for a 22-foot outboard cruiser that will pull water skiers, you had better settle for purchasing it complete.

However, several choices are open to the prospective builder, since boats can be constructed from many different beginnings:

1. You can build from plans and raw materials.
2. You can build from pre-planned, pre-cut material (otherwise known as a supplied kit boat).
3. You can buy an unfinished hull and complete the rest.
4. You can buy a finished hull and complete the rest.

As the hull is the most complicated part in the construction of the boat, and the one most likely to give you trouble unless your experience and confidence are consider-

Building versus Buying

able, perhaps it is a good idea to start with a finished (or nearly finished) hull.

Kit boats are becoming more and more popular every year. Much of the difficult cutting is done for you, and the plans are written step-by-step and can be followed easily. The initial cost of a kit boat is only about one third that of a new factory-built job. However, there are other expenses to consider: freight charges, extra hardware, and the power tools necessary to put the kit together. You will probably find that you will have to buy additional glue, filler, and sandpaper. Remember, too, that the cost of your engine should be taken into consideration as part of the over-all cost of the boat.

Although a kit boat does not take as much time to construct as a boat built from scratch, you will find that you must still devote most of your free time to its construction. An 8-foot pram takes on the average of 65 hours to build. A 10- to 12-foot rowboat would be completed in about 75 hours. A sport speedster in the 14- to 16-foot category would be built in 100 hours. The favorite 18-foot outboard cruiser would average 250 hours to completion, and a larger 22-foot outboard cruiser would take at least 300 hours of your time.

Another important factor to bear in mind about kit boats is that their resale value is considerably lower than that of a factory-built boat of the same age and condition.

A final and vitally important consideration is whether or not your personality is suited to the task. Assuming at the start that you are a good carpenter, can you follow instructions to the letter, or do you substitute and take short cuts? There are no short cuts in boat building. How much perseverance do you have? Are you easily discouraged? Everything is not going to go well every day. Will you rip out whole sections and rebuild to correct a small error? Will you continue long after you've lost the first flush of excitement? Have you the resources and patience to find just the right materials, the proper hardware for your boat, and to do the last beautiful finishing touches? If not, then give up the idea.

But if you like to paint, you can save about $400 by buying an unpainted cruiser and painting it yourself.

HULL FORMS

When you are shopping for a boat, bearing in mind the purpose for which you want it and the waters in which you'll operate it, you will need to understand the different kinds of materials, construction, and engines that will best suit your needs.

FLAT BOTTOM   V-BOTTOM   ROUND BOTTOM

Let's begin with the three basic forms of boat hulls: round-bottom, flat-bottom, and V-bottom. Each has advantages and disadvantages that are peculiar to it.

The round-bottom hull which comes down to us from primitive dugout canoes is the oldest form. In modern times it is usually found on more expensive boats, since it is more difficult to build; but it offers comfort and seaworthiness. Many commercial fishing boats have this type of bottom.

The flat-bottom hull is generally found on rowboats, and since it's easy to build, it is often used on homemade boats that are built without plans of any kind. The flat-bottom hull should be used only in very sheltered waters because it is extremely unstable in water that is at all rough. It is particularly suited to shallow-water operation. Most airboats (craft propelled by modified airplane engines) utilize a flat-bottom hull, skimming over heavily weeded and often very shallow water. They can hit 40 miles per hour, but their use is restricted to swamps and smooth waters because of the hull design.

The V-bottom hull is the most popular type for modern pleasure boats, combining as it does the good features of flat-bottom and round-bottom hulls. It is not hard to build and it is seaworthy. Since the sides of the hull come down to meet at the V bottom, there is more room inside the boat than in the other types.

Displacement and Planing Hulls

There are two types of hull design: the displacement and the planing hull. Both can have either a flat, round, or V bottom. The displacement hull rides deep in the water, and the boat is pushed *through* the water. Large boats are usually of this type. Flat-bottomed barges and tugs both have displacement hulls, as do round-bottomed canoes. Most ocean-going boats have displacement hulls, since a boat that rides deep in the water has more stability than one that rides the surface.

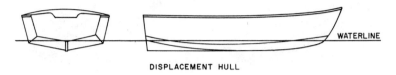

DISPLACEMENT HULL

A planing hull resembles a displacement hull when it is moving at low speed, but once it reaches planing speed, it lifts up and rides on top of the water. This happens because the forward part of the hull is a deep V, while back toward the stern the hull becomes flat and broad. As the boat

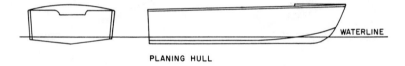

PLANING HULL

increases its speed, the hull keeps moving up until it is riding on its broad aft portion. In most boats this usually takes place at about 18 miles an hour, when the load is minimal. The amount of weight carried in a planing hull has a definite effect on its planing ability. It is much faster than the displacement hull, but harder to handle until it reaches planing speed.

Catamarans

The term "catamaran" means "multi-hulled" and is used to describe a boat with two hulls. The design originated in native canoes with outriggers attached to give added stabil-

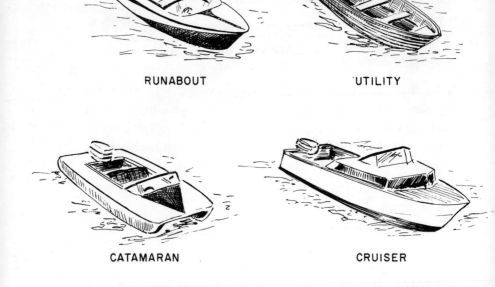

RUNABOUT

UTILITY

CATAMARAN

CRUISER

ity. When a single-hulled boat cuts diagonally across the wake of another boat, it tends to be forced off course. But in a catamaran, one hull helps stabilize the other. The wide beam of a catamaran affords a spacious deck which is enjoyable for sun bathing.

Catamarans have certain disadvantages, one of which is "porpoising." In choppy water and at high speed, air is captured between the two hulls, lifting the bow off the water. Single-engine power is not as efficient on a catamaran as on a conventional hull. Maximum efficiency requires a twin-engine installation.

Along with the hull design you should consider the matter of what material it is made of and how it is built. Deciding on material used to be simple; there were only two—wood and canvas. But today modern technology has given us a wide range of new materials ideally suited to boat building.

RUBBER AND CANVAS BOATS

Small life rafts and dinghies use rubber or rubberized canvas as a covering—excellent materials for this purpose, since the craft can be folded to take up a minimum of space. Repairing rubber craft is as easy as repairing an automobile tire, and most of them come equipped with repair kits containing all the necessary items. An inflatable raft is handy if you have to moor your boat away from a dock.

All canoes used to be covered with canvas, but now most of them are of lightweight aluminum. A canvas canoe requires painting every year, and the hull can be punctured easily. However, there is a certain beauty in a sleek painted canoe with the interior varnished to a luster, and it is worth the work it takes to keep it up.

WOODEN BOATS

Wood is still holding its own against all the new materials, partly because of its beauty. True, it requires maintenance, but many boatmen feel that keeping up a boat is as much a part of the sport as cruising.

Wooden boats come in two kinds: a carvel hull and a clinker-built or lapstrake hull. The carvel hull is completely smooth. Each plank is laid beside the other, much like a hardwood floor except that there is a slight spacing between the planks, to allow the wood to swell when placed in the water. The space, called a seam, requires caulking—a process by which you force cotton into the seam, then seal it by placing caulking compound over it. The advantage of this type of construction is that the wood is usually not expensive. Pine and fir can be used, although many such hulls are made of expensive teak or mahogany.

Carvel hulls are easy to repair; it simply involves putting in new planks where necessary. One of their disadvantages is that they require a great deal of maintenance. The seams usually need caulking every other season, and the boat must be painted every season. During storage, all wood-planked boats dry out and the planks shrink as the water evaporates. When you put the boat back into the water, it will leak for about forty-eight hours and must be watched carefully. It is often necessary to pump out the water that seeps in. Keep this in mind if you plan to buy a planked boat that has been in storage.

A carvel-planked hull is made of heavy wood because the planks must be sufficiently thick to hold the caulking material. This added thickness does not appreciably increase the strength of the hull, but it does add excessive weight.

In clinker-built or lapstrake hulls, each plank overlaps the one below it. They are very seaworthy, and many off-shore boats utilize this type of hull construction. These hulls are lighter than carvel-planked ones because the wood does not have to be so thick and they don't require caulking. In fact, when a lapstrake hull leaks, the only thing you can do is tighten the point where the two planks overlap. It requires

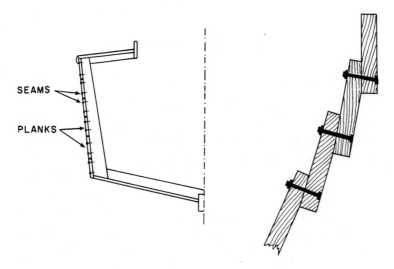

an expert repairman to work on a lapstrake hull, because of the difficulty of replacing a damaged plank; nevertheless, this type of hull is extremely popular.

Many people attribute the seaworthiness of a lapstrake hull to the small steps that trap air between the hull and water, thereby giving a better ride. The author can attest to the sturdiness of the hull because he raced a wooden lapstrake boat in a 260-mile race, half of which was in heavy offshore waters. The boat received more punishment in that race than a similar boat would receive in a lifetime of normal offshore use. Checking over the hull after the race, he found that only one plank had worked loose; and merely required tightening to get it back to its original condition. The author highly recommends a lapstrake hull if you plan to do much boating offshore and in rough water.

PLYWOOD BOATS

Plywood consists of thin sheets of wood glued together to form one thick sheet of four or five layers. It is important to specify that all plywood used in boat construction must be of the marine type. Marine plywood uses special waterproof glue that will withstand the destructive force of water. Since there is a considerable difference in cost between marine plywood and regular plywood, some people try to save money by using the latter in boats. They soon discover that all the effort that went into cutting and shaping the plywood was wasted. In one short season, the wood becomes warped and soggy and completely useless. An acquaintance of the author used regular plywood for a new deck on his runabout. He did a near-expert job, but after five months the wood had deteriorated so much that his foot went through the deck.

Two types of plywood are used on boat hulls: sheet and molded. Sheet plywood is used to cover an expanse of hull that otherwise would require six or seven planks to cover. This advantage, plus its superior lightness, has caused sheet plywood to replace planking as a construction material in small runabouts. With sheet plywood there are fewer seams to leak, and the hull requires fewer frame members to support the broad plywood than to attach to planks.

The disadvantage of sheet plywood is that it restricts the curvature of the hull, since the plywood can only be worked to a certain point. You'll notice that a sheet plywood boat does not have a flare to the bow and that the hull itself does not have any extreme bends or curves.

Sheet plywood is used a great deal in kit boat construction because it is easy to work. Repairs are easy too; anyone handy with tools can do a competent job. As added protection, fiberglass covering can be applied to a plywood hull. This lends strength and durability; unfortunately it also increases weight.

Molded plywood hulls are also lightweight, though more expensive than sheet plywood hulls. A molded hull is built in almost the same way as a sheet plywood; that is, layers of wood are glued together. First a mold of the hull is made, and a single sheet of wood, especially treated to conform to the contours of the hull, is placed over it. Waterproof glue is applied and another thin sheet of wood is put on, with the grain running across the sheet beneath it. This process is repeated six or seven times until the desired thickness is attained. Another matching mold is then placed over the first one and they are pressed together under high pressure. After the glue dries under pressure, the molds are removed, and you have a hull made of a single solid piece of plywood. Small runabouts with molded plywood hulls require no frame members, so they are light and require a minimum of upkeep. Without framework, the hull is flexible and will give as it cuts through the water.

Repairing a molded plywood hull is difficult. Even an

experienced repairman will have a hard job getting the hull back to its original appearance after it has been damaged.

ALUMINUM BOATS

It was shortly after World War II that aluminum made its first big impression on the boat-building market. It is lightweight and strong—two characteristics desirable in boat construction. Unfortunately much of the aluminum used at that time was obtained from salvaged bombers and was totally unsuited to boat construction. It oxidized rapidly in water and was not very strong.

The aluminum that is being used today is far superior to that used in the early postwar years. Its strength is attested by the fact that many world-record-breaking hydroplanes are built of it. Although oxidation is still a problem, a good coat of paint or one of the new plastic coatings eliminates this to a certain degree. The modern alloys resist oxidation well in fresh water, but the powdery substance that results from it increases in salt water. Still, with care an aluminum boat will last as long as any other kind.

The disadvantages of aluminum boats are that to some skippers their light weight makes them seem flimsy; and they are difficult to repair. Welding aluminum requires a skilled worker with special equipment. A dent is hard to straighten because the metal stretches, leaving a bulge after the dent is repaired. Rivets can be used in some repair jobs, but they are not pleasing to the eye.

An aluminum boat must be painted regularly, since the

paint wears off easily and the natural shiny surface gives too bright a reflection in the sunlight.

But otherwise you need not hesitate to buy an aluminum boat as long as it is sturdily constructed and is made by a reputable boat-building company.

STEEL BOATS

Aside from commercial and military uses, steel has not made an appreciable showing in boat construction. Undoubtedly it is rugged, but the corrosion factor is so high, especially in salt water, that it requires constant maintenance. But with recent advances in protective coatings and improved types of corrosion-resisting steel, it has a good future in hull construction.

On inland waters such as lakes and rivers, many steel cruisers are seen. For a small runabout the material is too heavy to warrant extensive use.

FIBERGLASS BOATS

Fiberglass has had a tremendous impact on boat building. It is a natural material because it doesn't need painting (most boats have the color mixed right in with the fiberglass), it resists damage from insects that prey on wood, and it doesn't rot, corrode, or absorb water.

Most fiberglass hulls are constructed much like the molded plywood hull discussed earlier. A layer of glass cloth is laid over a mold, polyester plastic resin is then applied, and another layer of cloth placed over it. This process is continued until the desired thickness is obtained. Fiberglass can also be molded to any hull contour. Unlike the molded plywood hull, the fiberglass hull can have defects as a result of this process. If the resin is not applied evenly, or there is a spot that is not covered, the hull may have a weak point which might result in hairline cracks. Reputable fiberglass boat manufacturers keep a close scrutiny on the lay-up process, but some small builders turn out fiberglass hulls that are not constructed properly. It's almost impossible to determine how well a new fiberglass hull has been made; you must rely on the reputation of the builder.

The buyer of a fiberglass boat shouldn't get the idea that the boat is indestructible or that it doesn't require maintenance. You can punch a hole in a fiberglass hull just as easily as you can in a wooden or aluminum hull. The advantage is that repairs are simple and can be carried out by anyone who can follow instructions. The ease and quality of a repair job on fiberglass is shown by the fact that it is almost impossible to tell where the damage was done after it has been repaired.

Although colors are impregnated into the fiberglass, a boat may need occasional touch-ups, especially on the topsides where the constant exposure to the sun may fade the colors. Anti-fouling paint must also be applied to the hull bottom. Unlike a wooden hull that requires painting for protection, the fiberglass hull and topsides are only painted to enhance the beauty of the boat.

Scratches are another problem with fiberglass, but

special compounds and waxes help to keep this to a minimum. Flotation, which is discussed in Chapter 3, must be installed in fiberglass hulls, as it must be in all construction materials that are not naturally buoyant.

TYPES OF POWERBOATS

Types of powerboats range from a small dinghy to an ocean-going yacht, but for the purposes of explaining them here, we can divide them into four basic types: runabout, utility, catamaran, and cruiser.

A runabout usually ranges from 14 to 22 feet in length and is equipped to carry passengers. It is designed for high-speed operation, and it usually has a planing hull. Outboard power is used predominantly, but there are quite a few inboard runabouts. The runabout can be compared to the sports car of the automotive field because it is fast and highly maneuverable.

The utility is an outboard or inboard boat primarily designed for fulfilling a certain type of job. Utilities have open cockpits equipped for a minimum of passengers. They can be called work boats because they have a lot of room that can be used to haul anything from people to petroleum drums. Today, many boats with a utility design are intended for pleasure and they give the owner seaworthiness along with spaciousness.

Catamarans fall in the same category as runabouts, but they have two hulls. They are fast, roomy, and stable. Their maneuverability is not as high as that of a single-hulled craft, but they are much more difficult to capsize.

Cruisers are enclosed boats ranging from 22 feet up. Most cruisers are equipped with bunks for sleeping, along with seating accommodations for passengers. Power can be either inboard or outboard.

SELECTING AN ENGINE

Once you've selected your boat, it's time to consider the problem of choosing the correct engine. Of course, the first consideration that comes to mind is speed; most of us want as much as we can get. And it is at this point that many amateur boatmen make their first big (and sometimes fatal) error. It is true that the more horsepower your engine carries, the greater its thrust will be. However, you must be sure that your boat is built to carry a powerful engine. A small boat with a too large engine is liable to break itself to bits before you get into midstream. What determines the kind of engine you choose is the boat you have chosen.

Motors, like boats, are suited to particular jobs. So once again consider the purpose your boat is to fulfill. Just as you wouldn't take a rowboat on a weekend cruise, so you can't expect a fishing motor to pull water skiers.

If your boat is primarily for fishing and you want it mainly for transportation to and from fishing areas, then choose one of the smaller engines—6, 10, or 15 horsepower— commonly called fishing motors and used on small boats of many shapes but usually under 14 feet in length. A small 10 or 15 horsepower motor can bring a small utility boat up

OUTBOARD PERFORMANCE CHART

HORSEPOWER		6	10	15	22	35	45	60	70	80	90	120	140	160
SMALL	Maximum Speed Without Skiers	18	25	28	32	33	35	38	40	42	–	–	–	–
RUNABOAT	Skier Capacity	–	–	1	2	2	3	4	5	6	–	–	–	–
LARGE	Maximum Speed Without Skiers	–	–	–	25	28	30	33	35	38	38	40	42	44
RUNABOAT	Skier Capacity	+	–	–	1	2	2	3	4	5	5	...6 OR MORE...		
SMALL	Maximum Speed Without Skiers	–	–	–	–	26	28	31	33	36	36	38	39	40
CRUISER	Skier Capacity	–	–	–	–	–	1	2	2	3	3	4	5	6
LARGE	Maximum Speed Without Skiers	–	–	–	–	–	–	27	28½	30	31½	34	36	38
CRUISER	Skier Capacity	–	–	–	–	–	–	1	1	2	2	3	4	5

to a speed of 30 miles per hour.

If you want more versatility, you'll have to look for a more powerful motor. A 22-horsepower motor can do anything a small motor can do, including trolling at 1 mile per hour. It can also pull one or two water skiers at a speed of 20 miles per hour or more—the speed necessary to keep them afloat. The larger 35 to 40 horsepower motors are a new category. These are general-purpose motors and will plane any type of boat up to and including smaller cruisers.

The larger cruisers can take advantage of the 60, 70, and 80 horsepower engines. These powerful motors give the boat great versatility.

How much power a planing hull can safely handle

depends on how sturdily the boat is built and how fast the particular model can be driven before it becomes skitterish, uncomfortable, and hard to handle. You can often tell when the speed limit is reached in single-engine planing-hull boats because the hull will begin to "porpoise," or gallop up and down rhythmically.

Consult the Outboard Performance Chart for speeds and capacities of the various horsepowers. This chart will aid you in estimating the maximum speed of family outboard boats using different horsepower engines, and the number of water skiers each combination will pull. These figures are based on the hypothesis that the boat is a planing boat of good design and is running with a light load. They are approximate and, of course, vary with the different hull designs, choice of propeller, gross load, and weight distribution. Wind and water conditions will also affect operating performance.

PROCEDURE FOR DETERMINING MAXIMUM HORSEPOWER

Most manufacturers specify the maximum horsepower that their boat will safely support. However, in the event that you do not know how large an engine your boat will carry without endangering its safety, there is a formula to follow that will give you the answers.

Multiply the over-all boat length by the over-all stern width. (Use the widest part of the stern. Use the hull length in feet and inches as measured from the stem face to tran-

How to Determine Maximum Horsepower

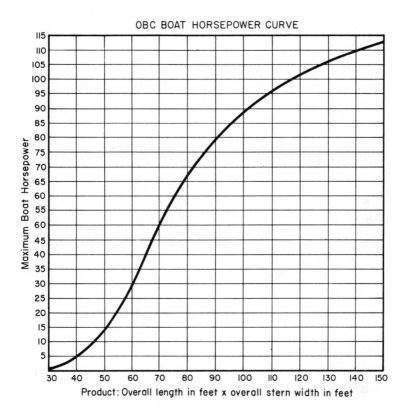

OBC BOAT HORSEPOWER CURVE

Maximum Boat Horsepower

Product: Overall length in feet x overall stern width in feet

som outside its highest point on a straight line parallel to the keel. Leave out any extending structures such as outboard brackets, fins, etc.)

On the horizontal axis of the Boat Horsepower Curve locate the exact point that corresponds to the answer arrived at. Follow the vertical line up to where it meets the curve. Read across to the vertical axis to find the equivalent point on the axis. Then take the printed number just above this point as the Maximum Horsepower for your boat (i.e., if the point on the vertical axis is 32, the printed number above is 35).

If you are considering a twin-motor installation, make sure your cruiser is built to take it. For twin-engine installation, your transom must be at least 6 feet wide, and there must be a minimum space between motor centers of at least 20 inches. A 22-inch center is greatly preferred. The greatest asset that such a twin installation offers is the extra measure of safety when cruising in large bodies of water. If one engine conks out, there is always a second to bring you home. There is no appreciable difference in speed gained between having one 30-horsepower or two 15-horsepower engines on your boat.

A new engine in the 15 to 75 horsepower range can cost from $300 to more than $1,000. The advantages of buying a new engine are obvious—the manufacturer stands firmly behind the engine; a new engine usually carries a guarantee and there is much less chance of a breakdown or dissatisfaction. However, you can save a considerable amount of money by purchasing—wisely—a used motor.

A USED ENGINE

When you buy a secondhand engine, you are starting out with a largely unknown quantity. You can't come back screaming when it breaks down . . . you can only blame yourself for picking a lemon.

There is a proper way to buy a used motor, though, and if you are considering it, you will find that you can actually save money and end up with a good engine if just a few precautions and check points are heeded.

CHECK THE COMPRESSION. Take the time to examine your prospective motor thoroughly. Turn the motor over slowly, using the starter or rope. Use fresh gasoline. If the engine starts smoothly without trouble, check the compression as okay. A good motor will have bounce and vitality. If it starts weakly, there is at least a ring problem, or perhaps badly scored cylinder walls or beaten-up pistons.

THE CRANKCASE. Check the armature plate for excessive oil accumulation. If you find it dirty, this is an indication of faulty upper bearing assembly.

CYLINDER CONDITION. Remove the spark plugs and, using a pencil flashlight, peer into the cylinder head. Check for excessive carbon accumulation, as this will affect the performance.

PROPELLER BUSHING. Exert up-and-down pressure on the propeller shaft and check for seepage around the propeller shaft seal. If there is excessive up-and-down play or seepage, it is indicative of a worn bushing.

FUEL LINE AND WIRING. Make sure that there are no breaks or cracks and that the wiring has solid connections.

LOWER UNIT. Drain off some of the lubricant and check it for foreign matter.

Final Check

Check the ease of controls, tilt locks, motor covers, and the general appearance of the engine. Just as boats deteriorate rapidly with poor maintenance, engines are quick to show signs of neglect. Check, too, the condition of the propeller. Make sure that the blades are free from scratches and mutilations.

Start the motor. Make sure it responds well to throttle acceleration and operates smoothly at full power. Check its ability to idle quietly. Turn off the engine and start it up again. Note whether or not it kicks over easily and powerfully. Make sure it will start smoothly.

It is important when buying a used motor to have an expert check it. Don't rely upon the seller's opinion. He may be an expert, but after all, he wants to make a sale. If none of your acquaintances is an expert mechanic, it will pay you in the long run to hire an expert to give the motor a thorough once-over before you spend your money.

YOUR TEST RIDE

Before making the final decision on what boat to buy, be it new or used, you must take a test ride. It's amazing how many people buy a boat they have seen in the dealer's showroom without actually trying it out. A number of important characteristics can be discovered on a test ride, and it's up to you to insist that the seller let you try the boat out or have him take you out in it. There are certain requirements a boat should meet, and even if you are a complete novice, you will be able to pick them out. Here are the six points to look for on a test ride:

1. Safety
2. Design
3. Seaworthiness
4. Versatility
5. Speed
6. Livability

SAFETY. This is the most important feature to look for in a boat you plan to buy. If the boat is a lightweight, 14-foot runabout with a massive 60-horsepower engine hung on the stern, beware! This is almost like putting an automobile engine in a kiddy car. Sure, it makes it go—and fast, too,— but the power plant is totally unsafe for the rig. Now, the same engine could be perfectly safe with an 18-foot runabout designed to take that amount of power. Check the outboard motor chart found earlier in this chapter to get an idea of the horsepower needed on the boat.

Equally important is the amount of flotation the boat has and where it is located. Wooden boats usually have enough natural buoyancy to keep them afloat if swamped, but fiberglass and metal boats must have flotation built into the hull. You can't expect the seller to fill the boat with water to see if it will remain afloat, but you can ask him where the flotation material is located and how much there is of it. The ideal location for foam flotation material is up under the gunwale and under the forward deck. A good 4 to 6 inches of the material should be present up beneath the entire underside of the deck. If the boat has sealed compartments as a means of flotation, there should be enough to support the weight of the boat and the passengers. Sealed-off compartments are not the best type of flotation because they can be punctured, and they consume precious room, but they are still better than nothing. Do not buy a metal or fiberglass boat unless it contains some type of flotation. Of course, you can install your own flotation by using the kits available on the market, but if you're spending your hard-earned cash for a boat, it should have the basic safety features. (For more on flotation, see Chapter 3.)

DESIGN. Naturally, you want a good looking boat—one that you will be proud to call your own, but don't make the mistake of buying a flashy runabout, all decked out with eye-catching doodads that add nothing to the performance of the boat. Elaborate tail fins are completely useless on a boat, even though the manufacturer may claim they add stability to the boat. In fact, they could hinder the performance of the boat by offering more wind resistance. While studying the appearance of the boat, take a look at the workmanship. You don't have to be an expert to pick out poor construction. Wood that is not finished smoothly or joints that don't meet properly are indications of poor workmanship. Study the construction carefully and you can get an approximate idea of the quality of the boat.

SEAWORTHINESS. Have the seller put the boat through a few maneuvers to get an idea of how it handles. Avoid a boat that feels flimsy or unstable as it is being put through its paces. Also, try to determine if the boat will hold up against the abuses of wind and weather. You are going to keep the boat in good condition, but if you start off with a boat that requires too much maintenance, you will lose a lot of your love for boating.

VERSATILITY. There is not one boat that will fill the requirements of all the uses you can put a boat to, but you can determine if the boat will fulfill more than one function. On your test ride, inspect the space to see if there is enough room to store water skis if you plan to participate in the sport. Think of how you are going to use the boat and see if the boat lives up to these expectations.

SPEED. This doesn't mean only how fast the boat goes; it also applies to having enough speed to handle the boat properly. You don't want a boat that drags through a turn or does not have enough get-up-and-go in choppy water. Speed is not only dependent upon the horsepower of the engine but also on the hull design. Therefore, try to determine if the boat has enough power, or maybe too much power, for the hull design.

LIVABILITY. Look over the boat and see how comfortable it will be when you own it. Is there enough room to have a folding cot or air mattress in the aft cockpit? Are the seats comfortable? Is there enough storage space? All these and many other questions should be answered on your test ride. Again, you must determine how you plan to use the boat before answering these questions. But make sure the boat fulfills as many demands as you will be making on it.

These six points are easy to remember, and if they are present in the boat that you are testing, consider it a good boat. At least you will feel more confident in your final choice of the boat to buy. Most boats will pass the test with flying colors; those that don't should be avoided.

FINANCING YOUR BOAT

For most of us, buying a boat will take more money than we have on hand at any one time. There is not only the cost of the boat itself, but the motor and—unless you live on the waterfront or pay dockage—a trailer to transport it. And so it may be necessary to find a means of financing your boat, as you would your automobile.

Many banks have come to realize that the widespread interest in boat buying can be good for their business, and they are offering various finance plans similar to those for buying automobiles and electrical household appliances. At present only 27 per cent of outboard motors and 32 per cent of outboard boats are being sold on an installment basis, whereas 60 per cent of electrical appliance sales and 55 per cent of furniture sales are financed. But installment buying of boats is increasing, and it's possible that you can find a bank in your area that will be interested in financing your boat.

Banks usually require you to make slightly larger down payments for outboard boats and equipment than they do for loans on appliances, but smaller down payments than they require for automobile purchases. Rates of interest for outboard boats and motors are slightly higher than for automobiles, slightly lower than for electrical appliances.

Most banks and lending companies require a down payment of 20 to 30 per cent of the price of the boat. The interest and the length of time for repayment may vary from one bank or finance company to another, with the amount of the loan. Terms may be arranged from three to thirty-six months, with the average at twenty-four months.

Check at your local bank to see if they have finance plans for boat; if not, perhaps they will be interested in starting one. Be sure to examine the terms of interest and repayment carefully.

INSURE YOUR BOAT

Just as you figure insurance into the cost of your car, you should include an insurance figure in the over-all cost of your boat. Your boat needs the same protection as your automobile. Boating policies, however, differ greatly from those for automobiles; they are usually figured for the specific amount of time that the boat is actually in use. For example, the insurance on your runabout would not be fixed at a yearly rate, but rather for the specific period of time you will be actually using the boat. The insurance is ordinarily written up for a one-year term and provides that the boat will be in commission for six months and out of commission for the remaining six months. The exact dates vary according to where you use the boat. In seasonal northern waters, the in-commission period is usually May 1–November 1. In warm southern waters, insurance usually runs for the entire year.

Most policies impose limits on boat operation. If you plan an extended cruise and will be outside of the water boundaries imposed on you by your policy, notify your insurance broker immediately and he will extend your coverage temporarily for the extent of the cruise.

Most boat insurance gives extremely broad protection which will cover just about all of your needs. The ordinary policy includes protection against liability for injury to anyone on the owner's boat or on any boat with which he may collide; against the cost of medical payments for any personal injuries; and against liability for the injury of anyone hired to work on the boat.

A policy covering outboard motors and boats is even broader than the standard yacht policy, in that the outboard motor is insured if it is dropped overboard. This policy usually covers all risks against physical loss or damages, with certain exclusions (freezing, wear and tear, mechanical breakdown, and inherent vice). It also excludes damage caused by repairing the boat or damage caused by anyone you may hire to repair or maintain the boat. Under this outboard policy, the company is not liable for more than the actual cash value of the property at the time of the loss.

If your outboard has a speed under 25 miles per hour, you may obtain liability protection from a landlubber policy known as Comprehensive Liability Insurance. This policy will protect you against claims for personal injuries occurring in and around your home, on a golf course, and most important, contains a clause covering liability when you are operating one of the slower outboards. If your outboard is faster than 25 miles per hour, a separate endorsement on this comprehensive policy can be obtained to cover you.

Under a normal policy you are not covered against losses resulting from the unseaworthiness of the boat . . . so make sure it will float and stay afloat. Keep your boat in good repair, as losses from wear and tear are not covered. Ordinarily a few other exclusions are stated in most policies —war risks, loss or damage to sails and spars while racing, etc. If an accident should occur, it is important to keep all evidence, since it is sometimes difficult to determine whether the accident is due to a peril of the sea (covered) or wear and tear (not covered). Many accidents are actually a combination of both. However, if you launch your boat in the spring and it sinks because the hull has dried out and the seams split, this is certainly due to your own neglect and is not considered to be a peril of the sea.

If you transport your boat to the launching area by trailer, you must obtain separate coverage for the boat while it is being transported. This is not normally included in the ordinary policy. Perhaps you can have it covered by means of an endorsement on your regular policy.

How Much Does Insurance Cost?

Here are some typical examples of the cost of insurance for boats not over ten years old in three different price ranges. The following figures include injury coverage up to $5,000 per person and up to a total of $10,000 per accident, and property damage (to someone else's property) up to $5,000.

Boat Value	Typical Insurance Premium
$ 1,000	$ 85
2,000	140
3,000	185

Special insurance policies are now available to owners of outboard boats covering almost every risk of physical loss or damage to the property insured. These also protect against legal liability for collision damage to other boats or structures up to $500 or the amount of the policy, whichever is greater. Typical annual rates for boat and/or motor run 5 per cent of their current valuation, with a minimum premium of $10. Annual rates for trailers run 4 per cent of their current valuation, with a minimum premium of $5.00.

CHAPTER TWO

The First Day
With Your Boat

Whether you've bought a sleek new cruiser, fresh, clean, and glistening in the sun, or a secondhand outboard badly in need of a paint job, or have just put the final touches on a build-it-yourself kit, this day—the day you have your own boat shipshape and thirsting for the water—will be one of the most exciting days of your life.

You will be tempted to jump in it and head for open water; but don't do it, any more than you'd drive away in a new automobile without first becoming familiar with the controls and learning how to drive. Instead, set this day aside to get acquainted with all the different parts of your boat and their functions, and to make sure you have observed all the safety procedures outlined in Chapter 3. Under some circumstances you might actually be violating the law if you have not done so.

Parts of the Boat

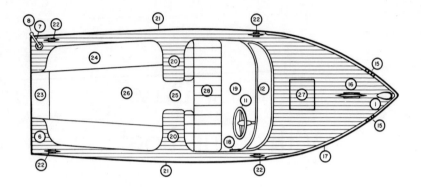

If you've bought a trailer, take the boat home and park it in your back yard and go over it inch by inch. You can do the same thing if your boat is dry-docked in a boat yard. If you are taking delivery in the water, squelch the desire to get underway, and make a thorough checkout of controls, steering, and other features.

Here is a diagram of a typical 16-foot outboard runabout. Study it closely so that you are familiar with these basic features of your boat:

1. *Bow light* . . . has two different colored lenses in it. The starboard (right) lens is green; the port (left) lens is red. The proper display of lights on a boat is very important and is discussed in a later chapter.

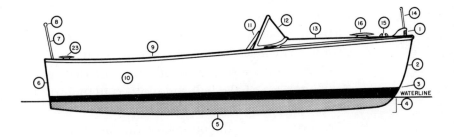

2. *Stem* . . . is the pointed part of the hull. It cuts through the water.

3. *Water line* . . . is a line painted around the entire hull which indicates the level where a properly loaded boat should ride in the water.

4. *Draft* . . . is the vertical distance from the water line to the bottom of the boat.

5. *Keel* . . . is where the sides of the hull come together at the bottom of the boat. It runs the entire length of the hull.

6. *Transom* . . . is the rearmost part of the boat and is usually constructed of heavier material than the rest of the hull. The outboard motor is attached to it.

7. *Stern staff* . . . is where the United States Coast Guard flag is flown. Only the Coast Guard flag may be flown from this staff.

8. *Stern light* . . . is the highest point on a runabout and must be visible from all positions around the boat. It is white. If your boat has a convertible or hard top that is higher than the stern light, then a white light must be installed on the hard top.

9. *Rub rail* . . . is a strip of wood or rubber that runs along the top of the hull and protects it from rubbing against the dock.

10. *Freeboard* . . . is the outside of the hull from the water line to the rub rail.

11. *Steering wheel* . . . operates outboard motor to turn boat.

12. *Windshield* . . . protects the driver from wind and spray. Safety glass or plexiglass should be used.

13. *Deck* . . . covers the forward part of the boat. The floor of the boat is sometimes also called the deck.

14. *Bow staff* . . . is where you can fly your own insignia or club pennant. It has no light on top of it.

15. *Bow chocks* . . . are metal fittings attached to the deck which guide the anchor line or mooring line.

16. *Bow cleat* . . . is heavy metal fitting used to secure anchor lines and docking lines.

17. *Toe rail* . . . is a strip of wood raised slightly above the deck. It helps keep you from sliding off a wet deck. On outboard runabouts it usually extends back to the windshield.

18. *Controls* . . . are usually composed of two levers,

one of which is the throttle and the other the gear-shift. Some later models have one lever for both throttle and gearshift.

19. *Cockpit* . . . is the area where the controls and steering are located and where the driver sits.
20. *Bulkheads* . . . are the vertical partitions separating various parts of a boat.
21. *Gunwale* . . . is a strengthening piece around the top of the hull. It is pronounced "gunnel." The edge of the boat is referred to as the gunwale.
22. *Mooring cleats* . . . are used to secure the aft section of the boat. These metal fittings are not as heavy as the bow cleat.
23. *Motor well* . . . is a compartment built under the outboard motor to catch water entering over the transom. A self-draining motor well has a hole at the bottom for the water to drain out.
24. *Stern seats* . . . are located in aft section of boat and provide seating for additional passengers.
25. *Walk-through* . . . gives access to aft section of boat. On larger craft it is called the companionway.
26. *Floor* . . . is platform supported above the bottom of the boat. It is sometimes referred to as the deck.
27. *Hatch* . . . gives access to the forward compartment of the boat. Many small outboard boats do not have either a hatch or forward compartment.
28. *Cockpit seat* . . . should be high enough to give the skipper a clear view.

As you progress in your boating knowledge, these terms will become a natural addition to your vocabulary. If you encounter a word with which you are unfamiliar, turn to the glossary at the end of this book; there you will find the definitions of commonly used nautical words.

THE CONTROLS

While the boat is still in dry dock or tied to a pier, climb aboard and sit at the steering wheel. There may be a small amount of play in the wheel due to the slack in the control cables. If there is too much, you may have to tighten the cables by taking up the slack. This is accomplished by loosening a screw clamp, pulling the cable tight, then re-tightening the screw clamp.

If the steering wheel is difficult to turn, inspect the pulleys to see if the cables have slipped. This happens frequently with cable controls and it should be the first thing you check when the steering is stiff. Once in a while the steering wheel itself will work loose, causing sloppy steering. Tighten the nut and bolt that hold the wheel to the dashboard.

Don't make the mistake of thinking that if you can drive a car, you can drive a boat. Many people do; they are the ones who head their boat directly into a dock and spin the steering wheel at the last moment, thinking the boat will respond as quickly as an automobile. If they're lucky, the result is a damaged hull; and it could be much worse. Remember that a boat steers from the stern (back), not from the front as a car does. When the outboard motor is turned it pushes the rear of the boat to the side, and the front in the direction of the turn. When you are operating a boat in close quarters, be sure to give the rear of the boat plenty of room, or you'll suffer the same experience as the novice who almost tore the transom off his boat when it caught on a bolt protruding from the dock as the boat pulled away. Give your stern plenty of clearance and avoid expensive repair jobs.

When you check over the steering, you'll notice that the outboard motor does not turn a full 90 degrees to the left or right, even though the steering wheel is turned as far as it will go. The construction of the engine does not permit this. Even if it did, the steering would not be improved, because the propeller would be attempting to push the boat completely sideways, therefore losing most of its efficiency to resistance.

If your boat is equipped with manual steering (an arm protruding from the outboard engine with a twist-grip throttle), the operation is somewhat different. To make the boat turn left, you push the motor arm to the right; to make the boat turn right, you push the arm to the left. Although the maneuver is simple, practice it a few times while the boat is still tied to the dock or at dry dock. Another thing to remember when operating a manual-steering boat is this—always sit facing forward. It is easy to have an accident when the skipper starts his engine and twists the throttle with his back facing the direction in which the boat is headed.

After you are familiar with the steering mechanism of your boat, the next step before actually getting underway is to inspect the controls and learn how they function. Most outboard runabouts have the steering wheel and controls located on the right side of the boat. The throttle and gearshift controls are usually placed in such a way as to make them handy for operating with your right hand. The control box has two levers protruding from it: the long one is the throttle and the small one is the gearshift. To make the boat go faster, you push the throttle forward.

When the gearshift lever is in the forward position, the propeller pushes the boat forward. When the gearshift lever is in neutral (in the middle position), the propeller does not turn even though the engine may be running. Always start your engine with the gearshift in neutral. When the lever is pulled back, the propeller turns in the opposite direction and pulls the boat in reverse.

Some control boxes have the throttle and gearshift combined in one lever. These units usually have a button on the side of the control box that, when pushed in, permits the throttle to engage the forward gear. When the button is pulled out, the throttle is combined with reverse gear.

Some control units even have electric push buttons for forward, neutral, and reverse. But regardless of the type of control mechanism your boat has, be sure you understand its operation before getting underway. The way you handle throttle and gearshift controls and the steering wheel in and around docking areas will indicate the kind of boatman you are. Banging into a dock, scraping the hull, overshooting the mooring, and sloppy boat handling in general indicate that the skipper is not very adept at handling the controls.

STARTING YOUR ENGINE

There is more to starting an outboard engine than turning on the key and pushing the starter. You will, of course, have fueled the motor and the auxiliary tank. The procedure and the safety precautions for fueling are explained in Chapter 3. Next, a number of last-minute checks must be made on the engine and the boat. These checks should be an everyday part of getting the boat ready before pushing the starter button or pulling the starter cord. The first thing to do upon entering the boat is to see if any water is in the bilge. If the boat has taken on some, due to last night's rain or through minor leaks, pump out the bilge until there is little or no water left. It doesn't have to be completely dry, but there shouldn't be so much water that it sloshes around the floorboards. Next, lower the engine from the tilt position. Make sure that the outboard motor is in the locked position after it is lowered. Double-check the lock by trying to lift the engine back to the tilt position. Connect the steering cables and control linkage if they have been disconnected. Check the connection to make sure they are secure and check the tension in the steering cables. Give the steering wheel a few turns to see if the motor responds readily.

Now you're ready to start the engine. While sitting in the helmsman's seat, put the gearshift lever in neutral. Advance the throttle slightly, turn on the key, and press the starter button. The engine should start if everything is in operating order. When starting the engine, use the throttle lever as though it were the gas pedal of an automobile.

Starting Your Engine

Once the engine is running, return to the stern of the boat and check if the water is coming out of the exhaust outlet on the lower unit of the engine. If there is no water mixed with the exhaust, it means the intake is clogged and the engine should be shut off immediately. Push the black button on the dashboard to stop the engine. Clean the intake hole and start the engine again. Once the water is present in the exhaust, you are ready to get underway.

If the battery is low or if you have a manual engine, you will have to start the engine with the starter rope. Follow the same procedure of making sure the gearshift is in neutral and the throttle is slightly forward. When pulling the starter rope, make sure you are braced firmly. Since it takes a hefty pull to get the engine turning, you may lose your equilibrium and go crashing to the floor. If at all possible, sit down when you pull the rope; if you must stand, set your feet wide apart. If the floorboards are wet or grimy, be extra careful.

In small engines that do not have reverse or neutral gears, it is important to face forward and to keep the boat headed toward open water when starting the engine. Since the propeller turns as soon as the engine begins to turn over, the boat will immediately move ahead. Be ready to grab the throttle grip of the steering arm as soon as the engine begins running.

To back up a boat that is equipped only with forward speed, simply rotate the motor 180°. You will notice when you back up that a wave of water will build up behind the transom and may splash into the boat. This is due to the resistance of the water to the wide flat board of the transom.

If you reduce speed when backing up, you can handle the boat more easily.

GOING ABOARD

Before you actually push off on your shakedown cruise, be sure you're properly dressed. You can do without brass buttons and a yachting cap, but it's important that your clothes and accessories be practical.

The first requirement is a pair of soft-soled shoes— sneakers. Hard-soled shoes can do as much damage to your deck as sandpaper on a varnished surface. Basketball and tennis shoes will protect your deck, but they may be slippery on a wet surface. It's worth spending a little extra to buy a good pair of yachting shoes to avoid scarring the finish of your boat and to prevent accidents.

Any close-fitting trousers and long-sleeved shirt will serve your purpose. Avoid loose-fitting clothes that could get snagged on a cleat or caught on your throttle lever. Denim and sailcloth are suitable because they dry rapidly. Wool is slow-drying and uncomfortable when wet, although a wool sweater comes in handy on a brisk day.

It's a good idea to keep a slicker aboard for protection against sudden rainstorms.

Don't overlook sunglasses or a visored cap—they can make all the difference when you're navigating directly into the sun. Keep in mind that the reflection of the sun's rays off the surface of the water can blind you and burn you as well as the direct rays; and navigational hazards such as floating debris are hard to discern in the sun's glare. Take your exposure to the sun in small doses. A bathing suit is great for swimming, but even on a cruise of a few hours, you will need more protection against the sun. Take along suntan lotion and additional protective clothing, or you may find yourself with a case of sunburn that will keep you off the water for several days.

There is a proper way to board a boat. When boarding from a pier or dock, step into the boat as near to the center as possible, keeping your center of gravity low. Don't leap; step surely and firmly, and pay attention to what you are doing, or you may find yourself in the water.

If you are boarding from a beach or a very high wharf, enter the boat over the bow. Make sure your tie lines are tight, or have someone on hand to steady the boat as you board.

Don't try to carry your gear aboard the boat. Place it on the pier in such a position that you will be able to reach it easily from the center of the boat. Step aboard and then reach back and pick it up. Better still, have someone hand it to you once you're safely aboard.

NEVER • jump into a boat
   • step on the gunwale (edge of the hull)
   • board with arms full
   • step on a slippery deck (use a step pad)
   • step into a boat that is pulling away from the dock

Before shoving off, there are some preliminary steps you should take to insure a safe and enjoyable cruise. The most important step is to make sure you have all the required safety equipment aboard. Look over the check list in Chapter 3 to see if you've left any safety items out. Once you have everything you need, pile it on the dock and systematically begin to load it on board. Keep in mind that all safety equipment should be accessible at all times. A life preserver stowed under a seat is too difficult to grab in case of an emergency.

In addition to the safety equipment, there are a number of other items you will want to take along on your cruise: spare engine parts, tools, extra gasoline, oil, and possibly a box lunch. As you begin to load the boat, you will find out what every boatman has discovered at one time or another in his cruising experience—there's just not enough room for everything you want to take aboard. This is especially true when you plan an extended cruise, but this won't come until you have put a number of miles under the hull.

Some boatmen load their outboards with enough gear to equip a large cruiser, then invite guests aboard and find that the boat is so overloaded that the water line rides beneath the surface. Be careful not to overload your boat. Sacrifice that extra duffle bag of clothing if you need the space for line or fuel.

Proper stowage of gear is one of the marks of a good boatman. He will have all the safety equipment readily accessible. All gear will be stowed neatly and will be secured so it won't break loose at the first sign of rough water. Lines will be neatly coiled, and bumpers and fenders will be located in a place where they will be handy when docking and out of the way when underway; never leave them hanging overboard once you pull away from the dock. Many boatmen, even experienced ones, forget to haul in the bumpers. This doesn't cause any damage to the boat other than possibly dirtying the hull, but it detracts from the trim appearance of your craft when you're underway.

With the gear all stowed neatly away, you are ready to shove off. Of course, you've made sure you have enough gas in the tank and in the auxiliary tank. Tell the dockmaster, a friend, or a member of your family where you are going and what time you expect to return. In case you get into trouble and there are no boats to offer assistance, someone will know where you are if you don't return to the dock when you are expected.

You've made sure the engine is operating properly and that water is coming out of the exhaust. Make a quick check of the fuel lines to see if any gasoline is dripping from them. The standard bayonet-type fuel connections have been known to leak if they are not attached securely.

While you are getting your boat ready for your first cruise, keep a sharp eye on the weather. If there are dark clouds on the horizon or strong gusts of wind, you had better postpone the trip. The first time out you'll have enough on your hands in learning the characteristics of your boat; don't ask for trouble by taking it out in foul weather. It may shatter your confidence to find yourself bobbing like a cork in a rough sea. If a sudden storm comes up while you are out, head into shore immediately, make your boat fast, and wait it out.

If you are starting out from a beach, push your craft out of the shallow water so the transom faces out toward the deeper water before starting up the engine. Otherwise, the engine prop will churn up mud from the bottom and clogging may result.

If you are setting out from a dock, first determine whether you are tied up to the "weather" or the "leeward" side of the pier. The weather side is the side the wind is coming from. If you are tied up to this side, cast off all lines. Turn the wheel hard over toward the dock to swing the stern out, then move ahead very slowly in forward gear for a few revolutions. Put the boat in reverse gear and back up far enough to get the boat clear of the dock, making sure that no boats are tied near you. Remember that the wind is against you and will be pushing your boat back to the dock, so be sure to swing the stern out far enough to make allowance for this. Let the person who is handling your line know exactly what you are doing at the wheel at all times. Call out each movement as you make it. When you are sure you are in the clear, shift to forward and head out to open waters.

If you're tied up on the leeward side (with the wind blowing from the direction of the dock) getting underway is much simpler. Start your engine and leave it running in neutral. Use an oar, boat hook, or your arms to push your boat away from the dock, and let the wind and waves carry you far enough to safely shift to forward. It is important to start the engine in neutral before pushing off; it is embarrassing to push off with a great "heave-ho" and loud "so long's" only to drift away with the wind and current when a temperamental engine won't start. Make sure it will start before you shove off—otherwise it can be dangerous as well as embarrassing! Don't stand on the foredeck unless your boat is constructed to carry weight there. Don't lean out over the side if you'd rather not find yourself in the water.

In all cases, be sure you have enough room for a turn when leaving the dock. If you don't, your stern will acquire numerous scars from engagements with the dock. It is easier and safer to pull out at a slight angle until you are well clear of the pier, then swing out into your turn. It will save wear and tear on your boat.

When leaving a mooring, be sure your engine is thoroughly warmed up before casting off. Check to see that no other boats are close to you—notice boats in the distance and their exact position. Determine whether the wind or the current is stronger by observing the direction in which your boat is heading. Cast off only when you are sure it is safe. Don't move ahead immediately after releasing your boat or you may run over your line and wrap it around the propeller. By reversing your boat until you can see the line you will be able to avoid it as you go ahead.

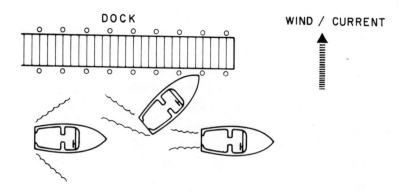

Backing out from a dock is better left until later, after you've become familiar with your boat and how it handles.

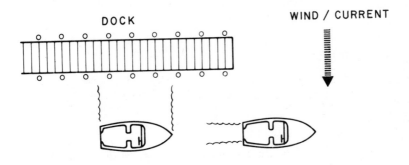

DOCK

WIND / CURRENT

UNDERWAY

Increase the speed of the engine while it is still in neutral and let it run for a short time. This will heat up the engine and prevent stalling as you maneuver away from the dock. Follow the procedure on pulling away from the dock, then head out to open water. Be sure there are no boats coming down the channel or none pulling away from the dock. Pull slowly away from the dock and keep this speed until you clear all mooring areas and channels. If you go too fast, the waves caused by your boat will rock the

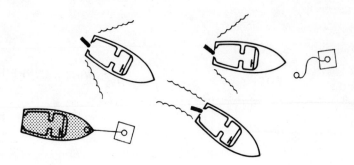

other boats tied to their moorings, and possibly cause damage. You are legally responsible for any damage caused by your boat's wake, so make sure you are in open water before you increase the throttle. If you have to pull around boats that are lying at anchor, be sure to give their anchor lines plenty of clearance to avoid running over them.

Once in open water, you will have the opportunity to get actual experience on the handling characteristics of your boat. Test your boat to see how it handles at various throttle settings. Don't attempt to take a turn at high speed; you can capsize the boat, or at best it will toss your passengers around. It's better not to take passengers on your shakedown cruise because they might make you nervous. If possible, have an experienced boatman accompany you. He will be able to point out your mistakes and give you sound advice on boat handling.

You will undoubtedly want to find out how fast your

boat will go. Don't attempt to give it full throttle unless the water is absolutely calm and there are no boats in the vicinity. Avoid making sharp maneuvers while at full speed. If the front of the boat rides too high at full throttle, you may have to drop the engine to the next lower angle. This is accomplished by moving the pin that determines the engine angle to the next lower slot. If the front of the boat seems to dig into the water, try raising the angle of the engine. You may have to rearrange the weight distribution to get the proper riding characteristic. As you progress in your boating experience you will learn just what weight distribution and engine angle are best for your boat.

You will want to know the cruising speed of your boat. This is the speed at which your boat gets up on the water and operates efficiently. It usually can be determined by giving the boat full throttle, then pulling back to about three-quarters throttle. Since each boat has its own cruising speed, you will have to experiment to find out at what throttle setting your boat operates most efficiently.

If the water is absolutely calm and you are in an open area, practice a few handling maneuvers. The fear of ramming into the dock or another boat won't plague you and you can devote your full attention to learning how the boat operates under certain conditions.

The first maneuver to execute is a circle. Reduce your speed and turn the steering wheel completely to the left or right. As your boat makes a complete circle, try to estimate the diameter of the circle in boat lengths. This is handy to know when you want to swing around in a narrow channel. You will notice the circle is slightly larger when you turn the wheel to the left. This is caused by the propeller turning to the right while the boat is turning left.

The next maneuver to try is backing up. Bring the forward progress of your boat to a halt by closing the throttle completely and putting the engine in neutral. When the boat is at rest, put the gearshift in reverse and advance the throttle very slowly. Bear in mind that steering will be more difficult because the wide transom is pushing against the water, and reduce your speed accordingly.

Now try reversing the engine while the boat is moving forward. Again close the throttle and put the gearshift in neutral, but before the boat comes to a stop, put the gearshift in reverse and increase the throttle very slightly. The bow will dig into the water and the boat will begin to back up. The faster the forward motion when you reverse the engine, the more violent will be the digging in of the bow. Never attempt to reverse engine while the boat is traveling fast unless it is an emergency. Even then, have the engine pointed directly forward; you might even turn over by reversing the engine while in a fast turn.

Another maneuver to practice is crossing a wake. Since you've picked an area that is free of other boats, you will have to supply the wake on which to practice. Increase your speed and take a wide turn so you can cut across your own wake. Approach the wake at an angle and reduce speed as you cut across it. If your speed is too great as you cut across the wake, the boat will lift up and come slamming down on the water.

You follow the same procedure when crossing the wake of a boat traveling in the same direction as you are. At a certain moment when you are directly behind the other boat, your engine will speed up and it will feel as though the propeller is slipping. Don't become alarmed for fear something is wrong with your engine. This sensation is caused by your propeller entering the slipstream of the propeller of the boat in front of you. Since the water is turbulent, your boat's propeller does not get a firm bite into the water and it increases in revolutions. Try to stay out of the turbulence caused by a boat in front of you, because it makes handling difficult and is not good for your engine.

If you have to leave the steering wheel for any reason either turn it over to a companion or stop the boat. Never leave the wheel unattended while the boat is underway. Many boatmen will reduce speed, dash to the stern to check the gas tanks, then return to the wheel. These few seconds are enough to run over a half-submerged log that could have been avoided if the skipper's attention were on the water in front of him.

The problem of floating debris is ever present to a boatman. He must search the water in front of him and avoid anything that bobs on or protrudes from the surface of the water. If you do hit a submerged object with the lower unit of the outboard engine, cut the throttle and shift to neutral. Check the extent of the damage, and if the housing is cracked, don't attempt to run the engine. Stop a passing boatman and ask him to tow you back to the dock.

If the submerged object punches a hole in the hull of your boat, immediately head for shore. Try to plug up the hole, but don't waste time. Head for the nearest land.

Floating debris is not the only obstacle you may encounter while skimming over the water. Always be on the lookout for hidden rocks, shallow water, strong currents, and other dangers. On inland waters you can usually tell shallow water by its color, which is slightly lighter than that of deep water. If there are ripples on the surface of the water not caused by the wind, it usually means shallow water or rocks beneath the surface. When navigating rivers, remember to take the longest route around a bend. Mud and sand bars are usually found on the inside of a turn.

Navigation off a coast or in the middle of a lake where the boatman will be out of the sight of land requires much more experience than the beginning boatman has. Never leave the sight of land unless you have a number of seasons of boating experience behind you and your boat is equipped with the gear necessary for offshore navigation.

While out on your shakedown cruise, you may feel like pulling up onto a sandy beach and taking advantage of that box lunch you brought along, or you may just want to let the engine cool down. Pick out a point along shore that has a gradually sloping sandy beach. As you near the beach, close the throttle, put the gearshift in neutral, and go to the engine and unlock it. Return to the steering wheel, shift to forward and slowly proceed toward the shore. Aim the boat straight toward land. As soon as the bottom of the engine touches ground, shift to neutral and kill the engine. The boat will gently glide onto the shore and the engine will be pushed up to the tilt position.

After the boat comes to a halt, tie a line to the bow cleat and secure the other end to a firmly implanted tree or rock. Keep an eye on the shore line to make sure the tide is not going out; you wouldn't want your boat left high and dry. This would be a good time to check how much gas you have remaining.

After your break, untie the line and shove the boat away from shore. Push the engine down and lock it. Follow the normal starting procedure and head out to open water. After completing your shakedown cruise, head into the dock.

HOME AGAIN

When tying up after an outing, the main consideration is the direction of the wind and current. Preparations for docking should be made long before you actually approach the dock. Tie lines should be in place and ready. Fenders to protect the boat from knocking against the dock should be put in place *before* you dock, not afterwards. Remember, too, that a boat has no brakes. Although a reverse gear can be helpful, a boat going forward will continue to move for some distance after you switch to reverse. Therefore, approach the dock as slowly as possible while still retaining control of the boat, and make allowance for some drift forward.

When the wind or current is behind as you approach a dock, make a turn to bring the bow into the wind or current (whichever is stronger) before you come alongside, if at all possible. You can use reverse gear to check forward momentum. If you must come in with the stern facing into the current or wind, be sure that you first kill your boat's headway by giving it sufficient reverse in time. If you secure the stern line first, the bow will drift in alongside the dock.

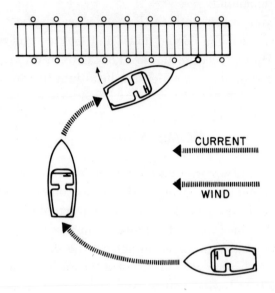

If the wind or current is coming from directly ahead, come into the dock at a 10° to 20° angle and secure the bow line first. The stern will then drift in against the dock.

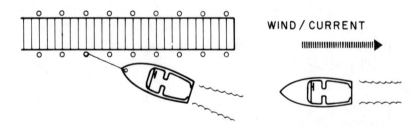

When the wind or current is carrying you toward the dock, simply bring your boat parallel to the dock and several yards out from it. The wind or current will gently drift your boat in alongside the dock.

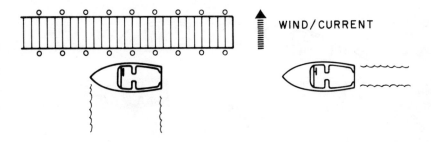

WIND/CURRENT

When the wind is off the pier, come in at a sharp angle until the bow touches the dock. Tie up the bow line and swing the stern around until you can tie it up.

WIND

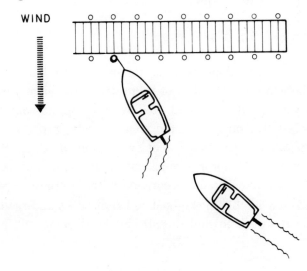

Mooring Procedures

When picking up a mooring, come up to it with the boat heading into the wind or current, whichever is stronger. Take a look at the other boats tied at their moorings to get

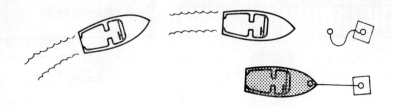

an idea of how the wind or current is affecting them. Approach your mooring in the same direction. Have a friend stand on the forward deck with a boat hook so he can pick up the buoy. Give him enough time to make the boat secure before you let it drift back.

If a crowded docking area forces you to back up against the wind or current in order to dock, cut down your speed as you approach so that you are in complete control of your craft. If you are on the weather side, bring your boat up parallel to and a few feet away from the dock. Be ready to give your motor a quick astern movement if any unexpected trouble should occur. With the stern in first, and a person available in the boat to handle lines and ready to hop on the deck to pull the aft end in, docking will be accomplished easily. After securing the aft line, grab the bow line and bring in the craft to dock.

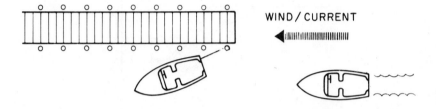

Making Secure

There is a right way of tying up your boat, too—and unless you want to see it hung up on the pier at low tide or adrift offshore, it is a good idea to take a few extra moments to tie up properly.

A simple bow and stern tie-up is recommended for *temporary* use. Use it on the lee side so that the waves don't pound the boat against the pier.

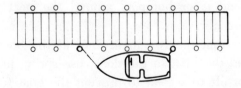

The angle method across an L-shaped or T-shaped dock is good both for temporary and permanent docking.

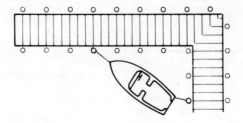

Using a pulley on a post compensates excellently for the wind, current, and tide action. Remember that when you are tying up in tidal areas you will need extra line to prevent a strain being put on your boat.

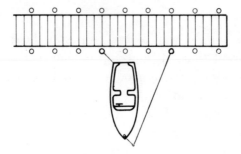

When tying up your boat overnight, be sure to place enough fenders or bumpers around the boat to prevent chafing and abrasions.

Aside from the two main lines at the bow and stern which hold the boat to the dock, use spring lines running forward or aft to a cleat to prevent the boat from yawing back and forth along the dock.

A final reminder: Where the water is rough or where you must contend with tides, leave plenty of slack in your tie lines.

CHAPTER THREE

Safety

Pick up a Sunday newspaper at the height of the boating season and you are bound to find a story describing a boating accident. These reports represent a small minority of boatmen. Since boating fatalities are rare, they invariably bring coverage, if not headlines, in the local press. Boating is still statistically safer than getting behind the wheel of an automobile and driving down a highway.

If this small minority used common sense and good judgment, boating accidents could be reduced by one half. The Outboard Boating Club of America made an extensive study of boating accidents and discovered that negligence—simple disregard for common sense afloat—accounted for almost half of the boating fatalities reported in one year. For example, more than one out of every ten fatalities was caused by someone standing up in a boat. Weather was another cause of fatalities, many of which could be attributed to bad judgment on the part of operators who set out in the face of bad weather or storm warnings.

Two of the major uses boats are put to are fishing and water skiing. You might think that skimming over the water on a pair of skis is much more dangerous than lounging in a boat with a fishing pole in your hand. Yet fishing accounted for over 40 per cent of the fatalities, while water skiing accounted for less than 2 per cent. The fact is that the fisherman is quite apt to stand in his boat, then fall overboard or unbalance the boat and cause it to capsize.

Young boatmen are not necessarily more accident-prone than older ones. Fewer than 3 per cent of the operators involved in serious boating accidents are under fifteen years of age. Of course, there are fewer operators in that age group; but the figure indicates that young people can operate a boat just as safely as older ones.

Take a look at the following table and you will see the cause of fatal boating accidents in one year.

CAUSES OF FATAL BOATING ACCIDENTS

Standing	10.9%
Poor observation	8.5
Unbalanced load	4.0
Sudden maneuver	6.8
Overload	3.4
Jumped overboard	3.7

Sudden starting	1.9	
Wake of another craft	4.1	
Hazardous waters	2.2	
Reckless operation	1.0	
Intoxication	1.4	
Miscellaneous	1.0	
Total accidents due to negligence		48.9%
Weather and wind storm	10.9	
Other conditions	.2	
Accidents due to natural phenomena		11.1
Engine fault or failure	1.8	
Unseaworthy boat	2.3	
Other mechanical failure	2.3	
Accidents due to mechanical fault		6.4
Faults not otherwise classified		1.9
Unknown		31.7
Total		100.00%

You can see that many of these accidents could have been avoided if the operator had followed the cardinal rule of safety—common sense.

SAFETY EQUIPMENT

You are required by law to have certain equipment aboard your boat depending upon its class. To know what this equipment is, you must know your boat's class.

Safety Equipment

> Class A—Any motorboat less than 16 feet in length.
>
> Class 1—Any motorboat 16 feet or over and less than 26 feet in length.
>
> Class 2—Any motorboat 26 feet or over and less than 40 feet in length.
>
> Class 3—Any motorboat 40 feet or over and not more than 65 feet in length.

It is important to remember that the following lists of equipment requirements for various classes are the *minimum* required to conform with the law. Don't be misled; you may need additional equipment to operate more safely.

Class A

(Less than 16 feet in length)

LIFESAVING DEVICES. You must have at least one Coast Guard approved life preserver, buoyant vest, ring buoy, or buoyant cushion in good and serviceable condition for each person on board.

Life preservers should be put on like a coat, with all ties and fasteners secured to obtain a snug fit. They will last for years if they are given reasonable care. They should be dried thoroughly before being put away and should be stowed in a handy place that is dry and well ventilated. Frequent airing and drying in the sun is also recommended. Life preservers should not be tossed around haphazardly, used as fenders or cushions, or otherwise roughly treated. In a small open boat, life preservers should be worn by children and nonswimmers. When rough or hazardous waters are encountered, every person should don a life preserver.

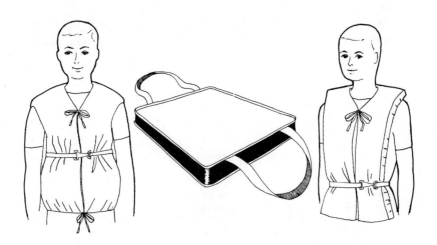

Buoyant cushions are normally used to sit upon, so they are always readily available in time of emergencies. However, they are difficult to hang on to in the water and do not afford as great a degree of protection as a life preserver or buoyant vest. For this reason, buoyant cushions are not recommended for use by children or nonswimmers. The straps on buoyant cushions are put there primarily for holding on, but they are also handy when throwing the cushion. The cushion should never be worn on the person's back as this will tend to force his face down in the water.

There are several types of vests; some are worn like a coat, others like a bib. Some have adjustable straps which should be adjusted to fit before going out. It's a good idea to try vests on children while they are in the water, to make sure the adjustments fit and performance is satisfactory. Vests should be worn snugly with all ties and fasteners pulled up tight.

Safety Equipment

LIGHTS. All boats are required by law to display lights at night. These lights warn others of the presence of your boat.

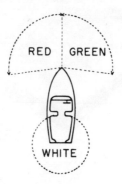

On Class A boats, a combination red and green light should be located in the forepart. It should show red to port (left) and green to starboard (right). It should be visible for one mile. A white light aft should show all around the horizon and be visible for two miles.

FIRE EXTINGUISHERS. Any fire extinguisher on board a boat must be of the Coast Guard approved type. If you are in doubt as to the approval status of your extinguisher, contact the nearest Coast Guard Marine Inspection Office. On a Class A boat you must have at least one B-1-type approved hand portable fire extinguisher. The types of extinguishers approved by the Coast Guard are carbon dioxide, dry chemical, and foam. Fire extinguishers containing carbon tetrachloride or chlorobromomethane no longer have Coast Guard approval, because the vaporizing liquids are toxic. It has been proved that inhaling the fumes of these extinguishers can lead to dizziness, or even death if inhaled to excess.

Remember, have your extinguisher checked at least once a year.

VENTILATION. You don't have to worry about this regulation if your boat is of open construction and powered with an outboard motor with a portable fuel tank. But if you have an inboard engine with an enclosed bilge and fuel tank, you must have two or more ventilators with cowls capable of eliminating fumes from the engine and fuel compartments. Many outboard boats are equipped with permanent fuel tanks; if your boat is one of these, you must have the tanks properly ventilated so the fumes pass overboard.

FLAME ARRESTORS. Again, this rule applies mostly to inboard boats. The carburetors on all gasoline engines, other than outboard engines, must be fitted with an approved device for arresting backfire. This regulation also applies to inboard-outboard installations where the drive is outboard and the engine is inboard.

BELL OR WHISTLE. Neither are required by law in Class A boats, but the Rules of the Road require that you give passing signals, regardless of the class of boat you have. Therefore, it would be wise to have a bell or whistle on board a Class A boat.

Class 1

(16 feet to less than 26 feet in length)

The same equipment required by a Class A boat is

required on this class boat. The only addition is a hand, mouth, or power-operated whistle or horn capable of producing a blast of at least two seconds' duration and audible for a distance of at least one-half mile.

Class 2

(26 feet to less than 40 feet in length)

LIFESAVING DEVICES. The requirements are the same as for Class A boats.

LIGHTS. This class differs vastly from the previous two classes in lighting. A white light must be shown in the forepart of the boat. A green light must be shown on the starboard side and a red light on the port side. At the stern there must be

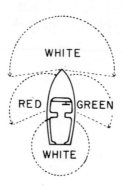

a white light showing all around the horizon and higher than the forward white light. The white lights must be visible for one mile.

FIRE EXTINGUISHERS. In this class you must have two regular-size approved hand portable fire extinguishers or one large-capacity approved hand portable fire extinguisher.

VENTILATION. Same as for Class A boats.

FLAME ARRESTORS. Same as for Class A boats.

BELL. A bell is required in this class, and it must produce a clear sound when struck.

HORN OR WHISTLE. You must have one hand-operated or power-operated whistle or horn capable of producing a blast of at least two seconds' duration and audible for a distance of one mile.

Class 3

(40 feet to not more than 65 feet in length)

LIFESAVING DEVICES. One Coast Guard approved life preserver or ring buoy for each person on board. Buoyant cushions or buoyant vests do not meet the requirements on this class boat.

LIGHTS. Same as for a Class 2 boat.

FIRE EXTINGUISHERS. At least three regular-size Coast Guard approved extinguishers or one regular-size and one large-size approved extinguisher are required.

VENTILATION. Same as for a Class 2 boat.

FLAME ARRESTORS. Same as for a Class 2 boat.

BELL. Same as for a Class 2 boat.

HORN OR WHISTLE. The boat must have a power-operated horn or whistle capable of producing a blast of at least two seconds' duration and audible for a distance of at least one mile.

The lights described in the above instances apply to inland waters. For boats operating on the high seas, there are International Rules governing lights. These rules can also be applied to inland waters. For a detailed explanation of lights and most other safety rules regarding pleasure boating, send for "Recreational Boating Guide," CG–340, U.S. Coast Guard. It is available from the Superintendent of Documents, U.S. Government Printing Office, Washington 25, D.C., at a cost of 40 cents a copy. This booklet contains everything there is to know about legal requirements for pleasure boats.

RECOMMENDED SAFETY EQUIPMENT

Coast Guard regulations indicate only minimum requirements. Here is a list of equipment that is not required by law, but helps to insure safer boating. Run down the list and check off the items you already have. Seriously consider getting those that you have not checked.

First-aid kit   Paddle
Portable spotlight   Fenders
Boat hook   Bilge pump
Extra oil and gas   Flashlight

Tools and extra spark plugs	Compass
Anchor	Charts
Extra line	Hull repair kit
Flares	Shear pins

This list can be expanded according to your own special needs. Keep in mind that the better you are prepared to meet emergencies, the less dangerous they become.

NUMBERING YOUR BOAT

Your boat requires a number just as your automobile requires a license plate. Boats propelled by machinery of more than 10 horsepower operated on the navigable waters of the United States must be numbered, regardless of length and whether fitted with inboard or outboard motors. Boats used exclusively for racing do not have to have a federal number.

Your state may have jurisdiction on numbering, provided its system is compatible with the federal system. Therefore you must find out what regulations are in effect in your state. For example, your state may require all pleasure craft, regardless of horsepower or type, to be numbered. For information on the regulations in your state, contact the local Coast Guard unit or ask your marine dealer.

If your state does not have a federally approved numbering system, you can pick up an application blank at your local post office. If your state has a federally approved numbering system, you apply directly to the state.

Once you get your numbers, it's important to display

them properly. The number should be painted on or attached to both sides of the bows. No other numbers are to be displayed in this area. Numbers should read from left to right, should be of block characters of contrasting color to the background, and not less than 3 inches in height. Remember, failure to have on board the necessary certificate or to properly exhibit the numbers subjects the owner or operator to a $50 penalty for each violation.

FUELING SAFETY

An ounce or two of loose gasoline can be one of the most dangerous hazards aboard a boat. It takes as little as 2 parts of gasoline vapor mixed with 98 parts of air to make a highly explosive mixture. Even the smallest spark or flame is enough to start a gasoline fire. As you can see, it is extremely important to use the utmost care when fueling your boat.

Outboard boats don't pose too much of a problem in this respect because the wise skipper has his portable tank filled on dock and not while it is in the boat. The open construction of most outboard boats allows enough circulating air to clear the area of gasoline fumes. But caution still must be used, especially when pouring fuel from the auxiliary tank to the portable tank while the boat is rolling in the waves. Wrap a rag around the spout of the auxiliary tank so the dripping will be absorbed. Have the engine shut off during the entire operation. Wipe up any gasoline spots, then rinse with water. Make it a habit to check your fuel lines on each and every trip.

Fire hazards are always present in an enclosed boat with a permanent fuel tank. Many outboards come equipped with permanent tanks; if your boat is one of them, make sure the tanks are installed properly and well ventilated. The best type of installation is a filler pipe firmly attached to the deck and extending to the bottom of the tank. The ventilation pipe should discharge the gasoline fumes into the open air, away from all hull openings, hatches, doors, windows, or ports. The outboard end of the ventilation pipe should be screened.

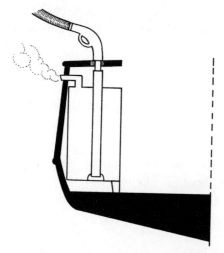

Keep the following rules in mind when fueling your boat and you will reduce the hazards:

1. Tie the boat securely to the gasoline dock.
2. Check to be sure that no one is smoking, about to light a match, or about to throw a switch.

3. Stop all electrical appliances such as radios, fans, motors, or other devices that could produce a spark. Never take on fuel with the engine running.
4. Avoid fueling at night, but if you must, turn off all lights and make sure the galley stove is out.
5. Make a quick check of the fuel system and estimate how much gasoline you will need. Never let an attendant fill the tank to the brim.
6. Close all cabin openings such as doors, windows, ports, and hatches.
7. During fueling, make sure the nozzle of the hose or can is in contact with the filler pipe to guard against static sparks.
8. Have a full fire extinguisher close at hand.
9. Make sure no fuel spills.
10. After fueling, replace and tighten the gas cap.
11. Wipe up any gasoline spilled and wash down with water.
12. Open all windows, doors, ports, and hatches to ventilate the boat for five minutes.
13. Make sure there is no odor of gasoline anywhere on the boat before starting the engine.

FLOTATION MATERIAL

Many boatmen incorrectly think that flotation material is a minor consideration to the safety of their boats. Without sufficient flotation, a boat can become a death trap if it is capsized or swamped. The proper amount of flotation is as important to the safety of your boat as a fire extinguisher or a life preserver.

The natural buoyancy of wood may lead you to think that a wooden boat will float regardless of the size of the hollow in the hull. But when that boat is loaded with hundreds of pounds of gear plus the weight of the engine and passengers, the natural buoyancy may not be sufficient to keep it afloat.

How much reserve flotation is required to keep a boat afloat? This is a difficult question to answer because it almost requires that you take your boat out to shallow water, sink it, and find out just how buoyant it is. Fortunately, the Outboard Boating Club of America has come to the aid of boatmen by giving them a formula by which they can determine how much reserve buoyancy is needed to keep a swamped boat from sinking. The basic OBC formula for flotation is:

$$F = \frac{W}{B}$$

F = the cubic feet of flotation material needed
W = pounds of flotation required
B = buoyancy of flotation material used, in pounds
      per cubic foot

To arrive at these figures, it takes a lot of calculations that could become confusing. To simplify the problem, let's take a 16-foot fiberglass runabout and figure out how much flotation material is needed to make it safe. Say the boat weighs 600 pounds. Four passengers and all the equipment including motor weigh 1,400 pounds. Therefore, the total dry weight of the rig is 2,000 pounds. Remember this is dry weight. When the rig and passengers are submerged in the water, the weight is reduced to about one third, or 700 pounds. Therefore, the 16-foot fiberglass runabout will need some type of flotation material that will support 700 pounds. Assume that Styrofoam is used. It has a buoyancy of 55 pounds per cubic foot; therefore if we substitute these figures in the formula, we get:

$$F = \frac{700}{55} \text{ or } 12.7 \text{ cubic feet of Styrofoam}$$

To be safe, it requires 12.7, or better, 13 cubic feet of reserve flotation to keep the 16-foot fiberglass runabout floating with four passengers hanging onto it. This flotation can be placed anywhere in the boat, preferably up under the decks and gunwales. Placed here, the flotation material will help to keep the swamped boat righted.

To assume that all 16-foot fiberglass runabouts with four passengers require 13 cubic feet of flotation material is a mistake. The total weight of each rig can vary tremendously, and the type of flotation may not be the same.

How, then, can you know if the boat you are buying has enough flotation? You can't, but you can rely on the specifications given by a reputable manufacturer, and you can check the boat yourself to see if there is an ample amount of flotation. Well-known boat manufacturers who have high safety standards usually install enough flotation in their boats. Be wary of buying a fiberglass, steel, or aluminum boat from a manufacturer who makes no mention of the type and amount of flotation material contained in the boat. Wooden boats usually have enough buoyancy unless they are overloaded with extra equipment. If you plan to buy a wooden boat that does have extra flotation built in, you can rest assured the boat is safe.

Plastic foam, air chambers, and balsa wood are some of the materials used for flotation. They have a high buoyancy and are excellent for this purpose.

If you have purchased a used boat that you think needs extra flotation, you can install it yourself by using one of the many flotation kits offered on the market. In some cases, the flotation material can be used to strengthen certain weak construction points in the boat.

The safety factor of sufficient flotation is not measured by the fact that it prevents you from having a complete loss if your boat is swamped or capsized. Knowing that you have something to hold onto in case your boat does swamp is of much more value. A number of drownings occur when occupants leave their boats and attempt to swim to shore. They fail to realize that the shore, even though it may be in sight, is much farther away than it seems. Never leave a swamped boat and attempt to swim to shore. Hang onto the boat until help arrives.

ARTIFICIAL RESPIRATION

Everyone in or around water should know how to render artificial respiration. You may never have to use it, but it's always better to be prepared for any emergency that may arise. The fact that it can save a person's life is enough reason to become familiar with the procedure.

Artificial Respiration

Suffocation occurs when breathing stops for any physical cause. The most frequent causes of stopping of breathing are drowning, electrical shock, and gas poisoning. Death will result unless breathing is started quickly. Even a few seconds' delay in starting artificial respiration may result in death.

Blueness of lips or suspension of breathing are the symptoms by which the need for artificial respiration may be recognized. The patient's mouth should be cleared of any obstruction, such as chewing gum or false teeth. There should be no interference with the air passing to and from the lungs. Artificial respiration should be continued at least four hours without interruption, until normal breathing is established or the patient is pronounced dead by a medical officer.

The mouth-to-mouth technique is an excellent method to stimulate breathing in a victim. Some first-aid kits contain a special tube to aid in the mouth-to-mouth method. Instructions for its operation are included, and they also explain how to render the mouth-to-mouth technique without the tube. Here is a brief description of the steps to take in the mouth-to-mouth technique:

1. Place the unconscious victim on his back so you can look into his face.
2. Move the victim cautiously.
3. If there is foreign matter visible in the mouth, turn his head to the side, force his mouth open and quickly clean the mouth and throat with your fingers or a piece of cloth.
4. Place the victim's head as far back as possible, and

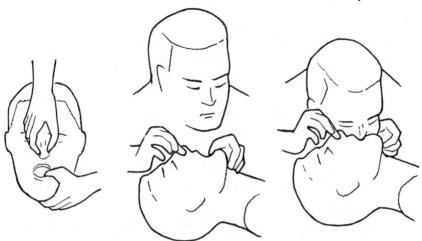

hold the lower jaw upward. It is important that the jaw is held in this position.

5. Holding the jaw in this position, approach the victim's head from *his* left side.

6. Insert the thumb of your left hand between the victim's teeth and grasp his lower jaw.

7. Lift the lower jaw forcefully upward so the lower teeth are higher than the upper teeth.

8. Hold the jaw in this position as long as the victim is unconscious.

9. Close the victim's nose with your right hand.

10. Take a deep breath and place your mouth over the victim's mouth, with an airtight contact. Do not hold the victim's mouth open too wide because you must take the entire mouth of the victim inside your lips.

11. Blow into the victim's mouth, forcefully if an adult and gently if a child.

Artificial Respiration

    12. While blowing, watch the victim's chest. When the chest rises, stop blowing and quickly remove your mouth from the victim's mouth. Let him exhale passively.

    13. Repeat the inflation 12 to 20 times a minute, or once every three or four seconds.

As soon as the victim is breathing by himself, or when additional help is available, see that his clothing is loosened or removed, if wet. Cover him with a blanket or clothing to keep him warm, but do not interrupt the rhythm of the artificial respiration. If he begins to breathe, adjust your timing to assist rather than hinder his breathing.

The Holger Nielsen, or Back-Pressure, Arm-Lift method of artificial respiration, is one of the forms adopted by the Department of Defense, U.S. Public Health Service, American Red Cross, and other national organizations on recommendation of the National Research Council.

Place the victim in the face-down position. Bend both his elbows and place one of his hands on the other. Turn his head to one side and place his face on his hand. Quickly clear his mouth of any obstruction and bring his tongue forward. Kneel at his head, on either knee, facing him. Place the knee close to his head. If it's more comfortable for you, kneel on both knees, one on either side of the victim's head. Place your hands on his midback, just below the shoulder blades. Fingers should be spread downward and outward, with thumb tips about touching.

Rock forward until your arms are vertical, and allow the weight of the upper part of your body to exert slow,

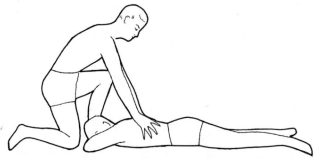

steady, even pressure on your hands until firm resistance is met. This compresses the chest, forcing air out of the lungs. Your elbows should be kept straight and the pressure exerted almost directly downward. Do not exert sudden or excessive pressure.

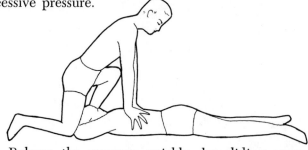

Release the pressure quickly, by sliding your hands from the victim's back without giving any extra push with the release. Now rock backward and allow your hands to come to rest on the victim's arms, just above the elbows.

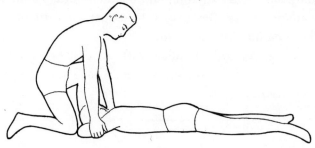

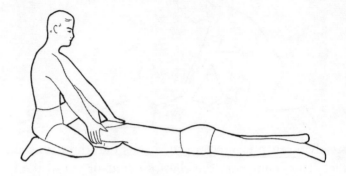

Continue rocking backward, drawing the victim's arms upward and toward you. When doing this, do not bend your elbows. Keep your arms straight, and as you rock backward, the arms of the victim will be drawn upward and toward you. Put enough lift on the arms to feel resistance and tension at the shoulders. The armlift pulls on the victim's chest muscles, arches the chest, and air is thereby sucked into the lungs. Lower the victim's arms. You have finished one full cycle. Repeat this cycle about 12 times per minute to the rhythm of:

1. Rock forward   3. Rock backward
2. Press   4. Stretch

Maintain a slow, easy rhythm, and continue until spontaneous breathing starts. Remember to adjust your timing to assist the breathing of the victim.

Become thoroughly familiar with at least one method of artificial respiration. It may someday save the life of a relative or friend.

COURTESY MOTORBOAT EXAMINATION

If you want to know if your boat is safe, request a Coast Guard Auxiliary member to make a courtesy examination. If your boat is awarded a decal, you can rest assured that your boat is safe. This boat check is made by qualified members for the purpose of acquainting you with the legal equipment requirements and other equipment recommended for greater safety afloat. There is no charge for this examination, and if your boat fails, it is not reported to the Coast Guard. You are not forced to do anything; you are only requested to rectify any safety violations.

Here's how to obtain a courtesy examination. If you know an Auxiliary examiner, make an appointment with him to have your boat inspected. If you don't know one, look in the local telephone book or write to the Marine Inspection Officer of the nearest Coast Guard district office for instructions. Once an appointment has been set, prepare your boat by having all the equipment ready for inspection when the examiner arrives. Don't have a crowd of people on your boat during the examination. The examiner will want to work efficiently, and the people will just get in his way.

The examiner will have a printed check list that he will check as he goes over your boat. The whole procedure should take about thirty minutes. If your boat passes, the examiner will affix a decal on the windshield which signifies your boat is safe, and the Coast Guard will refrain from boarding the boat unless violations are apparent. If your boat fails the examination, as one out of five do, the examiner will tell you what is wrong and how you can correct the violations. After making the necessary improvements, you can request another examination.

Don't think that merely having the prescribed safety equipment is enough to pass the examination. The most important part of the examination is checking the equipment required by law, but it goes further. Examiners will not award a decal to a boat that is not in over-all good condition. Dirty bilges, poor fire extinguishers, and faulty life-saving devices are a few of the things that could fail a boat.

Some of the items the Auxiliary suggests you have on board are: bilge pump, compass, course protractor or parallel rules, deviation table, distress signals such as flares, dye markers, mirrors, or flashlight, dividers, emergency rations, emergency drinking water, first-aid kit, Light List booklet, lead line, local charts, mooring lines, extra supply of motor oil and grease, ring buoys, r.p.m. table, spare engine parts, and tools. You can see that a boat must be well equipped to win an Auxiliary decal.

ORGANIZATIONS DEDICATED TO SAFE BOATING

The Coast Guard Auxiliary also offers an Outboard Motorboat Handling course consisting of one lesson, designed primarily for outboard operators, with the main emphasis on safety. It covers the fundamental rules on boat handling, equipment requirements, and the common sense rules of courtesy.

Safe Boating is a three-lesson course in the elements of seamanship, aids to navigation, rules of the road, and boating safety for both outboard and inboard motorboat operators. The course may be presented in three weeks, one week, or in one day, depending on the Flotilla offering the course. Included in it are lectures and demonstrations using color slides, models, and sound films. Booklets summarizing the course material are also available.

Basic Seamanship and Small Boat Handling is an eight-lesson course which provides a comprehensive but practical study of boating, covering seamanship, aids to navigation, piloting, rules of the road, safe motorboat operation, and accident prevention. Those successfully completing the course are awarded the U.S. Coast Guard Auxiliary Basic Smallboat Seamanship Certificate.

If you are interested in any of these courses, write to the Director of the Auxiliary located in your district or contact members of the Coast Guard Auxiliary Flotilla nearest you.

Another organization that is equally enthusiastic about boating safety is the U.S. Power Squadron. This nationwide association of boatmen conducts an extensive program of boating instruction. Their basic course, called the USPS Piloting Course, consists of twelve lectures that are designed to teach the student as much about boating as time permits.

The piloting course, offered free to the public, usually runs for twelve to fourteen weeks, and requires about three hours of classroom lectures or field training a week. The lectures are held in high schools, libraries, municipal buildings, or any other handy public meeting place. The field training is conducted at a nearby boating center. You'll have to do homework which is turned in at each lecture, but you'll enjoy it because it covers your favorite subject— boating. The material covered in the course is taken from textbooks issued by the national headquarters. After completing the entire course, you may take a written examination. If you pass, you are given a certificate. Many of the people who pass the piloting course are invited to join the local squadron; membership is not automatic.

After the piloting course, interested boatmen can continue with an advanced program and elective courses. The advanced-grade courses include seamanship, advanced piloting, junior navigator, and navigation. With each course you pass, you are awarded a higher grade of membership. Today, the United States Power Squadron numbers over 50,000 members making up more than 300 local squadrons.

You can't become a member of the USPS until you are eighteen years old, but if you are sixteen or seventeen and pass the piloting course, you may be accepted as a squadron apprentice. This is not a rule; it is up to the discretion of the local squadron.

Aside from the eighteen-year-old age limit, the USPS only requires that the person interested in becoming a member is dedicated to furthering the aims and objectives of the USPS, and that he is the type of boatman who will receive the maximum benefit from the educational programs.

You can be sure that a boatman who is a member of the USPS is keenly aware of all the safety practices of boating. For the time and place of USPS classes in your area, write to the Squadron in your area, or write to U.S. Power Squadron Headquarters, 96 West Street, Englewood, New Jersey.

Safe Boating Organizations

Many local chapters of the American Red Cross offer instruction in various phases of boating, ranging from canoeing to sailing. Their swimming courses are a must for any potential boatman who cannot swim.

The Boy Scouts of America and the Girl Scouts of America both have excellent courses in boating. Anyone who belongs to these groups should investigate the possibility of furthering their boating knowledge through the instruction offered.

One organization that has done the most to promote better boating is the Outboard Boating Club of America. Supported by the pleasure boating trade, the OBC has the safety and enjoyment of boatmen as its primary aim. Each year it puts out a multitude of booklets, pamphlets, and printed literature, all directed to helping the boatman. Its activities range from offering teaching courses in boating to drafting model state boating laws. If you ever need any boating advice, write to the Outboard Boating Club of America, 307 North Michigan Avenue, Chicago 1, Illinois. If they can't help you, they'll tell you who can.

Before you or any member of your family take out your boat, you should become familiar with the laws of your state covering the operation of motorboats.

New York State has passed a law stipulating that young persons under ten years of age may not operate a power-driven craft on the waters of the state unless they are accompanied by a person over fourteen years of age. The law further requires that children from ten to fourteen must hold a boating safety certificate before they are allowed to operate a boat alone. This certificate is issued after a boy or girl has successfully completed a four-hour safety course. The course is not designed to teach boat operation, although this is covered to some extent. Although the law mentions specific ages, the course is open to older children and to adults.

If you live in New York State or a state that offers similar courses, you should attend these classes. For information on them, write to the Motorboat Division of your state Conservation Department, or inquire at your city hall or police station.

If your state does not offer courses for boatmen, then it is your own responsibility to acquire the necessary knowledge of safety rules and procedures.

SAFETY CHECK

As a review of some of the safety points covered in this chapter, here are twenty suggestions for safe operation:

1. Do not overload your boat.
2. Do not leave shore in a leaky or poorly constructed boat.
3. Observe the pilot rules.
4. Instruct at least one of your passengers in the rudiments of handling your boat in case you should become disabled, and, without alarming them, see that all passengers know what to do in an emergency. Show all passengers where the emergency equipment is located.
5. Obtain local information and familiarize yourself

with the locality in which you are going to operate
your boat. Do not venture into dangerous or restricted waters.

6. Have lifesaving devices readily available and wear
   them when conditions warrant.
7. Check the weather and tides before going out, and
   have due regard for them.
8. Make sure gasoline tanks are properly installed.
9. Bilge should be free from oil, waste, and grease.
10. Electrical equipment and wiring should be in ac-
    cordance with safe marine practices.
11. Have an adequate fuel filter.
12. Check your battery and its ventilation.
13. Do not operate the boat near swimmers.
14. Do not use gasoline stoves.
15. Always provide life belts for children and be sure
    they wear them.
16. Don't be afraid of your boat—respect it.
17. Don't forget that the wake of your boat can dam-
    age others.
18. Always reduce speed through anchorage areas.
19. Don't lie at anchor with a short line; allow suffi-
    cient scope.
20. Make sure you have all legally required equipment
    and that it is in good operating order.

COURTESY—THE KEY TO SAFETY

A courteous person is a thoughtful person, and a

thoughtful person is a safe boatman. The simple rule of treating your fellow boatmen the same way you would like to be treated will go a long way in making you a safe boatman. The reputation of a nautical hot rodder or reckless boatman spreads like wildfire in a boating community, because most of the inhabitants are dedicated boatmen who want to realize the full enjoyment of the sport without having to worry about fools who endanger that pastime. Most of the restrictive legislation pertaining to boating has resulted from that small minority of boatmen who have no respect for their boats or their fellow boatmen.

Some of the resentment sailboat enthusiasts have toward "stinkpots," as they call powerboats, is well founded. Some motorboat operators get a thrill out of speeding through dockage areas and making as much noise as possible with their engines. Outboard engines are never completely quiet, and the use of full throttle should be avoided when it is disturbing, especially at night.

Probably the largest single complaint one boatman has against another is the nuisance and damage caused by the boat's wake. Although the offending boatman is liable for all damage incurred by the wake of his boat, the damage is often not extensive enough to warrant a legal suit. You're not going to go to court over a scraped hull or gouged rub rail resulting from the boat bobbing up and down against the dock when a boat speeds by, but this doesn't prevent your becoming angry when it happens. Have you or your guests ever tried boarding a boat while it was rocking at the dock? If you have, you know how irritating it can be. This alone should make you conscious of the necessity for reduced speed when passing docks or mooring areas.

Outboard manufacturers claim that their engines do not disturb fish, but what about fishermen and their lines? A speeding boat will cause a wake that will rock a small fishing boat as though it were on the high seas. The poor fisherman has all he can do to hang onto the gunwale and shake his fist at the violator. Running over fishing lines invokes even more anger from the fisherman. Always keep clear of fishermen; if you must go near them, check the angle of their lines entering the water so you will be sure to avoid cutting and tangling them with the propeller.

Another violation of good manners afloat is boarding a boat with hard-soled shoes. If you are ever invited aboard a boat while you are wearing street shoes, slip them off. You won't offend anyone, least of all the skipper.

Litter on the beaches and waterways is as unsightly as litter lining the nation's highways, but it is more dangerous when floating on the surface of the water. Litter in the form of floating debris has accounted for damaged propellers and rudders. To combat the problem of the litterbug-boatman, some yacht clubs have issued stiff penalties to anyone decorating the docks and mooring areas with beer cans, soft-drink bottles, paper plates, and other debris.

Here are a few reminders about nautical littering. Always carry a travel trash bag or container on board, and bring the bag back to port for proper shoreside disposal. Dispose of trash while afloat only in legal deep-water areas far out from harbors and shore fronts, and then only in closed and weighted containers which will sink to the bottom. Garbage bags are not to be used because they quickly disintegrate when immersed in water. Make sure you puncture both ends of a can so it will sink. Always clean up picnic areas and campsites so trash will not be blown into the water. If you've learned to curb the urge to toss that piece of paper into the water, you've taken a step toward becoming a courteous boatman.

CHAPTER FOUR

Seamanship

The dictionary defines seamanship as "skill in navigation," but the term has come to mean much more. When a pleasure boatman speaks of seamanship, he usually means the whole range of activities performed while on board his boat. To practice good seamanship, a boatman must know all facets of boating from Rules of the Road to rope handling.

RULES OF THE ROAD

Although the amount of traffic on the waterways is small in comparison to that on the highways, there are traffic laws governing the operation of boats. These marine traffic laws—known as rules of the road—vary according to the locality in which you operate your boat.

Rules of the Road

There are four different sets of rules:

1. Great Lake Waters
2. Western Rivers
3. Inland Waters
4. International Waters

The rules sometime require different lights, whistle and horn signals, and even different passing maneuvers. Boats operating on the Great Lakes and their connecting tributary waters as far east as Montreal must follow the "Rules of the Road for the Great Lakes," as contained in Coast Guard pamphlet CG–172.

Boats operating on the waters of the Western Rivers must follow the rules of the road as contained in Coast Guard pamphlet CG–184. The Western Rivers include the Mississippi River and its tributaries.

The rules of the road for boats on the Inland and International Waters are contained in Coast Guard pamphlet CG–169. If you operate your boat on the rivers, harbors, and other inland waters, except those covered by the Great Lakes and Western Rivers rules, you use the Inland rules. Boats operating on the waters outside the boundaries of the United States, normally called the high seas, are bound by the International Rules of the Road.

You can get whichever pamphlet you need from the local Coast Guard Marine Inspection Office.

The basic purpose of all the rules of the road is to let one skipper know what the other one is doing. These rules apply to the skipper of a small runabout as well as to the captain of an ocean-going liner.

Although the following explanations and illustrations apply to inland waters, they are similar to the other rules of the road and will help in explaining them. You are still urged to study and follow the rules pertaining to your sphere of operation.

Meeting Another Boat

If a boat is heading directly toward you or nearly so, bear to the right and let the other boat pass you on the left (port) side. A good way to remember this rule is to imagine that you are driving an automobile. As you do in an automobile, keep to the right when someone is heading toward you. The rules state that you must give a short blast of your horn of one second duration as you prepare to pass the oncoming vessel.

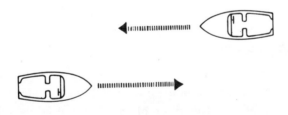

If the boat that is heading toward you is off to your right, you're not going to make a sharp right turn in order to pass him on your left. What you should do is give two short blasts of your horn and proceed along your present course. Under this circumstance you are permitted to have the oncoming boat pass on your right (starboard) side.

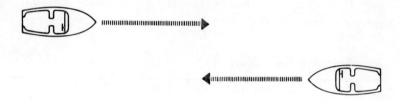

As simple as these rules are, there can still be much confusion when the situation arises. You may think the other skipper will not observe the rules, so you turn in the opposite direction. To avoid this confusion, start the maneuver as soon as possible; don't wait until you are almost on top of the other boat.

Crossing Situation

When two boats are approaching each other at right angles or obliquely, which might result in a collision, the starboard boat has the right of way, and it is called the *privileged vessel.* For example, if you're cruising along and a boat appears off to starboard (on your right), you must slow up and give him the right of way. You are called the *burdened vessel.* Make sure to cross his wake astern of him. Each boat should give one short blast of its horn to make sure the other understands. If the boat that has the right of way slows up or any other misunderstanding occurs, sound four or more short rapid blasts on your horn. This means both boats should stop and back up if necessary. Do not proceed until both you and the other operator are clear as to what each of you is doing. Remember that four or more short, rapid blasts of a horn mean danger. When you hear them, always slow up or come to an immediate stop.

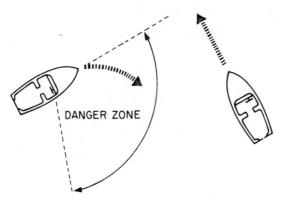

DANGER ZONE

Overtaking Situations

When you are overtaking (passing) another boat, it is your responsibility to give the proper signal. As you come up to a boat and overtake it on the right, you must give one short blast on your horn. The boat that is being overtaken should answer with one short blast of its horn. If you overtake the boat on the left, you must sound two short blasts on your horn, and the overtaken boat should answer with two short blasts. If the boat ahead of yours sounds four or more short, rapid blasts of the horn, do not attempt to pass, for it means it is unsafe to pass. You should only overtake a boat when your signal is satisfactorily answered.

If you are in the boat being overtaken, you should maintain the same speed and course while the boat behind you passes. It's much like passing in an automobile, except signals are given. And as in an automobile, the skipper of the boat overtaking another does not cut the boat short. Also, if you are being overtaken, do not cross the bow or crowd upon the course of the passing boat.

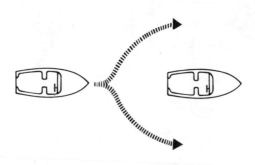

It is important to remember that it is the responsibility of both skippers to be on the alert and take every precaution to avoid an accident. There's no way of knowing if the skipper of the other boat will follow the rules of the road, so it's up to you to be constantly aware of his maneuvers. If he is not following the proper course of action, it's up to you to get out of his way. This is especially true when navigating in rivers and harbors where commercial traffic is heavy.

Although the rules of the road apply to water-borne vessels of all types, from small runabouts to large ocean-going ships, it is important to realize that a large ship is much more difficult to maneuver than a small pleasure craft. Common sense tells you that it would be stupid, as well as dangerous, if you insisted on your rights in navigation. When operating a small pleasure boat near large ships and commercial towboats, the best rule to follow is to "stay clear." A large ship has certain areas, called blind spots, where the skipper's vision of the water around him is obscured or completely blocked. Never assume that the skipper of such a ship can see you in time to avoid a collision. It can take from several hundred yards to a mile to stop a large ship.

The propellers of a large ship are also a source of danger. They can create a strong surface force that could swamp your boat or even pull it under the surface. Stay as far away as possible from the stern of a large ship.

Another place to exercise caution is on rivers where barges are tied along the waterway. Strong river currents rushing beneath a moored barge have been known to pull a boat underneath it. If you must launch or land your boat near a moored barge, be sure to do it downstream from the barge.

When meeting a commercial tug pushing a string of barges around a bend in the river, remember that the stern of the tug slides around the bend. Steer clear of the tow even though it means you are violating the rules of the road. The tug usually has to navigate that particular place in the river because the skipper may be staying in a channel. He can't get out of your way, so it's up to you to get out of his path.

Locking Through

Locks are passageways on a dam that permit boats to navigate from one level of water to another. There are many different types of locks, but all of them function as an elevator that lifts or lowers a boat. Navigating a lock is not difficult if you know the basic rules: follow the lockmaster's signals, have the proper equipment, and use caution.

Signals vary with different locks, but they all have the same reasoning behind them. They tell the skipper when it is safe to enter the lock. Many locks have signals similar to those found on a highway intersection. A red light means stop, do not attempt to enter the lock; yellow means caution; and green means to proceed to the lock. Entering the lock requires a very slow speed—about 6 to 10 miles per hour. Fenders, bumpers, or other hull protection should already be in place. Have at least 50 feet of sturdy line ready to toss up to the men working on the walls of the lock. As added precaution, it is wise to have two lines, one from the bow and one from the stern.

As the water level of the lock rises or lowers, keep an eye on the possibility of the hull's rubbing the lock walls. Also be keenly aware of the boats around you; the surging of the water into and out of the lock can make the boats bob around. Once the all-clear signal is given by the lockmaster, slowly proceed out of the lock. Do not resume cruising speed until you are well clear of the lock doors.

Although locking through is a simple procedure, it can be dangerous if the skipper is negligent and does not observe the proper rules. For assistance in river navigation, specifically locking through, write or visit the Corps of Engineers in your district. They will supply you with handy, informative booklets on river navigation.

Other Applications of Rules of the Road

When a powerboat and a sailboat are proceeding on a course that might result in a collision, it is the responsibility of the powerboat skipper to keep his boat out of the way of the sailboat. A sailboat in this sense is defined as a boat relying on sail alone for power. If the sailboat is overtaking the powerboat, it is the responsibility of the sailboat skipper to keep clear of the powerboat. In fog or weather that causes poor visibility, a boat should proceed at a moderate speed. The Supreme Court has defined a moderate speed as a speed no greater than will enable a boat to stop in half the distance of visibility. This means that if you can see 100 yards in the fog, you must maintain a speed that will permit you to stop the boat in 50 yards.

AIDS TO NAVIGATION

Just as the rules of the road are the traffic laws governing boats, the aids to navigation are the traffic signs. One of the most important of these traffic signs is the buoy. The color, shape, number, and other characteristics of a buoy tell the boatmen how he may avoid navigational hazards and help him to follow a safe course. There are three basic shapes of buoys: nun buoys, which are shaped like a cone; can buoys, which are shaped like a can or drum; and the spar buoys, which are shaped like tapered poles.

Nun buoys are always red and have an even number painted on them. Can buoys are always black and have an even number on them. Spar buoys can be either red or black and have either odd or even numbers on them. The red nun buoys are always on the right side of the channel when proceeding upstream, and the black can buoys are always on the left side of the channel when proceeding upstream. If the spar buoys are black, they are on the left; and if they are red, they are on the right. Upstream means traveling toward the source or headwaters of the channel from seaward. Many boatmen use the three R's of navigation (red, right, returning) to remind themselves that red buoys are kept to the right when returning from the sea (upstream). Conversely, when traveling downstream (toward the sea) the opposite rule applies.

In addition to indicating the channel, buoys are used for many other purposes. Buoys with red and black horizontal stripes mark an underwater obstruction or junction with another waterway. If the top stripe is red, it should be considered a red buoy. Keep it on your right as you proceed upstream.

Buoys with black and white stripes mark the center of a channel. Pass close by it on either side. All white buoys mark the entrance to an anchorage area.

It is important to remember that buoys are not immov-

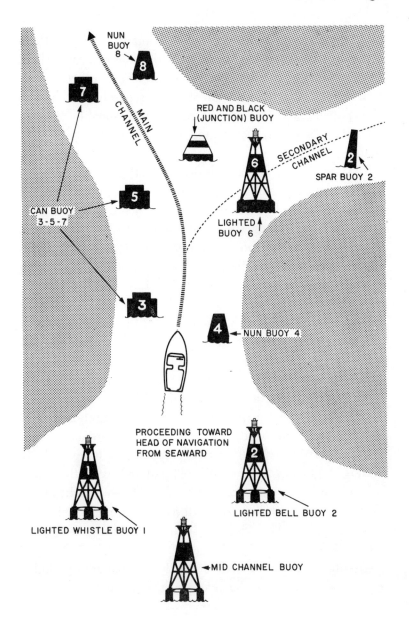

NUN
BUOY
8

7

RED AND BLACK
(JUNCTION) BUOY

SECONDARY
CHANNEL

SPAR BUOY 2

MAIN
CHANNEL

5

6

LIGHTED
BUOY 6

CAN BUOY
3 - 5 - 7

3

4 ← NUN BUOY 4

PROCEEDING TOWARD
HEAD OF NAVIGATION
FROM SEAWARD

1

2

LIGHTED WHISTLE BUOY 1

LIGHTED BELL BUOY 2

← MID CHANNEL BUOY

able objects. Although every effort is made to anchor them securely, storms, unusual tides, and collisions can cause them to come adrift, to be missing, or to be off the charted position. Even buoys that are on station (securely anchored to the spot intended) should be passed a reasonable distance off, since they may be located near the obstructions they mark.

Many of the other aids to navigation, such as lighthouses and lightships, will not be encountered by the novice boatman, but this is no reason for not being familiar with them. All along the coasts of the United States and along some of the interior waterways are towering lighthouses, placed where they will be of most use in warning the boatman of dangerous waters. They may be painted with stripes or in a solid color, to distinguish them from the background. The light that comes from them is given a distinctive characteristic so it can be easily identified. Lighthouses may have manned or automatically operated lights; in addition to the visual aid they render, they are usually equipped with fog and radio-beacon signals.

Lightships serve the same purposes as lighthouses and are similarly equipped. They mark the entrance to important harbors as well as dangerous shoals lying in busy waters. Lightships are usually painted red, with the name of the station in white on both sides. When a lightship is underway or off station, she will fly the International Code signal flags PC. This indicates that she is not at anchor on her station.

Minor light structures are painted similarly to lighthouses. They indicate the sides of the channel.

Range lights are usually small or skeleton structures which, when lined up (one over the other), indicate that the boatman is on a safe course. They are usually visible in only one direction. Steer a course to keep these lights in line and you will remain in the channel. Range lights may be white, red, or green. They may be steady or flashing.

Day beacons are aids to navigation. They may consist of a simple single pile with a daymark on the top. They often mark the sides of the channel. Many day beacons have reflectors to facilitate locating them at night by means of a searchlight.

NAVIGATION

Navigation is the science of conducting a vessel on the water from one location to another, and determining its geographical position. You will find that certain equipment is essential to navigation, and unless your boat is properly equipped, you will never be a good pilot. The first item that should be considered "a must" is a nautical chart for the water areas in which you plan to cruise. Navigating without a chart is even worse than setting off in an automobile to go across country without a roadmap. To help you in the use of your chart, you will need a course protractor, or parallel rules, a pair of dividers, and pencils and paper for figuring.

Navigation depends a great deal on visual observation of landmarks on shore. Rain and fog play havoc with visibility, however, so when this happens, good navigators rely on a compass to return to shore and harbor. Keep your compass near the controls of your boat. Make sure it is properly cushioned against damage from vibration. Also, see that it has a deviation card computed to show its error for accurate navigation under all circumstances.

Nautical Charts

Nautical charts are your most important tool for plotting a course, determining position, and accurately measuring direction and distance. Every hazardous reef, rock, or obstruction is marked on this chart. Buoys and lights are marked, and dangerous and restricted areas are clearly defined.

It is a good idea to purchase your charts early in the season. You will be able to give the proper amount of time to studying them, and just the thought of going cruising will be entertaining. Take your charts with you every time you go out in your boat. You can never tell when you will need them.

The Compass

Make sure that your compass is located in an area free from large steel objects and strong electrical fields for at least 12 inches in all directions. Keep your radio, direction finder, or other electrical devices at least 3 feet away from your compass.

A compass points to the *magnetic north*. This is actually some distance away from the *geographic* North Pole, which is the one used on charts and maps to indicate *true* north. The difference in direction between the geographic North Pole and the magnetic north is called *variation*. The amount of variation changes according to where you are located. Some charts show magnetic north right on them, but make sure the chart you are using is up-to-date, because magnetic north may change slightly from one year to another in some localities.

To adjust or compensate for this variation error, select a true magnetic north-south course and a true magnetic east-west course, by using a chart. Place the boat at the center, where the courses intersect. Make sure that the compensators are in a neutral position. (You may use a brass screwdriver, brass coin, or other nonmagnetic tool to turn the compensators.) Follow these steps to make the adjustment:

1. Placing your boat on a known north magnetic heading (0°), use the N-S compensators to adjust the reading to 0°.
2. With your boat on a known east magnetic heading (090°), use the E-W compensators to adjust the reading to 090°.
3. With your boat on a known south magnetic heading (180°), use the N-S compensators to reduce the shown error by one-half. Correct reading is 180°. If your compass shows 184°, for example, reduce error by one-half to 182°.
4. With the cruiser on a known west magnetic heading (270°), use the E-W compensators to reduce any indicated error by one-half. Correct reading is 270°. If your compass shows 266°, adjust to read 268°.

5. Repeat all four steps. When you place your boat back at the north heading, the compass may not read 0° any longer. If not, reduce your error by one-half, then follow the same procedure with east, south, and west. Continue until all error is removed. If all error can't be removed, your problem is one of deviation.

There is a difference between *deviation* and *variation* in a compass. Variation is a constant error in all magnetic compasses. Deviation is an error caused by the magnetic effect on your compass of anything in your boat that is made of iron or steel. You will find that deviation varies with different boats as well as with different directions in which any one boat may be headed. If deviation is your problem, make up a deviation card. To do this, make a check of compass readings for at least every 30° from north, all around for the full 360°. You can also make a check by comparing your readings with similar readings with a compass that either has no deviation error or for which an accurate deviation card already exists.

RIVER CRUISING

River boating has a special excitement all its own. More and more enthusiasts are taking to the rivers for their boating enjoyment. Navigating your boat on the river requires a special knowledge . . . a special ability to "read" the river.

Watch for mud or sand bars at the mouths of streams

where a secondary stream or river flows into a larger river or a lake. When the smaller river meets the huge body of water, the sediment that it is carrying usually settles to the bottom. When you are passing the mouth of a secondary river, stay well out in the main stream. If you are entering the secondary stream or river, look for the main, steady stream of water and follow it, ignoring the more settled waters on the sides. The quick-running water will cleanse the channel of the secondary river. The same rule holds true when emerging from the secondary river. Watch for floating debris or half-submerged logs or snags, especially at the mouths of rivers.

The deepest water on a straight stretch of river is usually dark in color and is found in the center of the river. The safest rule in river boating is to stay in the deep river water. When you come to a bend in the river, you will notice that the deep water almost always will be found on the outer edge of the curve, next to the highest bank. Try to stay in the channel where the water runs the swiftest and the river bed is eroded to the greatest depth. As water becomes shallower, it becomes lighter in color and has a tendency to ripple easily in a breeze. If you come across light, rippled water, stay away. You will find, however, that shallow water that is infested with weeds will not ripple easily, as the weeds tend to hold it steady. Beware of water that is speckled with weeds, as not only may they entangle your propeller, they may be in water only a few inches deep!

Keep a sharp lookout for swirls, eddies, or rough water suddenly appearing in the current. The chances are that they indicate an obstruction underneath the water. Patches of water that appear flat and calm are dangerous, too. They are usually indicative of a shallow spot in the river bed.

OFFSHORE BOATING

There are a few general rules of good seamanship that will help the offshore boatman, too. You must take special care as the sea and surf can create unique problems.

1. When running into strong headseas, always meet them at an angle instead of head-on. You will find that you will have a greater control of your boat and will have much more stability.

2. A cure for rolling in the trough of a heavy sea is to steer a zigzag course so that your boat spends only a short time in the trough when turning.

3. Many offshore boating problems are created because the boat is being run too fast. If your boat yaws (swerves from side to side) while running before a sea, you are probably going too fast. Slow down and let the seas pass underneath you instead of trying to outrace them.

4. When you are about to enter a strange inlet, hold back and see if any local boats are going in. If so, let them go in ahead of you. If not, stand off until a big sea (usually every third wave) comes along. Then run *behind* it through the inlet.

TOWING A BOAT

Helping another fellow is a basic rule of good boating. You will find that there will be times when you will be called upon to assist another boat by towing it to shore. If the water is rough, be sure to use a long tow line. Adjust the length so that the boat you are pulling rides on the crest of the wave, not in the trough. Make sure that the tow line is secured firmly to a side cleat or bitt. Try not to use the one on the stern of the boat, as your steering will be slightly impaired if you do. On most boats there is a towing ring, located on the stem (bow or bowsprit, forward). Always attach the line to the towing ring on the boat to be towed. If there is no towing ring, attach the line to the bow cleat of the boat to be towed. The occupants of the boat being towed should sit toward the stern. Never sit on the bow of a boat while it is being towed, because this will force the bow into the water, making towing much more difficult. Keep the rudder or outboard engine straight.

Just as a passing note of caution, if a fellow boatman asks you to tow him into shore, make sure he tosses his line to you. In some legal actions where damage has resulted to the boat being towed, the boatman who has offered the tow has been found responsible for damage to the boat. If the boatman who is in trouble throws you his line, however, you will be in the clear.

BE WEATHER-WISE

"Everybody complains about the weather, but nobody does anything about it"... except the boatman! What he does about it certainly doesn't change the weather, but it makes his boating happier and safer. The boatman must always know what to expect in the way of wind and water, so learn to read a barometer, develop the habit of looking at the sky, study cloud formations, and become familiar with local weather peculiarities. The good boatman never tempts fate by venturing forth in bad weather.

If you notice thunderhead clouds piling up in the sky and an ominous darkness falling over the water, stay ashore. If these conditions arise when you are out in your boat, head for the nearest shore and shelter. If a sudden squall surprises you, order any passengers you may have aboard to sit on the floor boards and keep the center of gravity low and reduce wind resistance. Then head into the wind and waves at low speed, making sure to keep enough headway so that the boat holds her course. If, for any reason, your engine should stop, drop anchor (leave plenty of line) and lie low until the storm blows over.

Take advantage of all the weather information that may be available to you. Listen to the forecasts on the radio whenever possible. Many newspapers, especially in boating areas, publish daily weather maps which are based on the Daily Surface Weather Map issued by the U.S. Weather Bureau. These maps may sometimes also be found on your post office bulletin board, at a Coast Guard station, or at the local airport.

Don't let your first glance at one of these weather maps cause you to panic. They will probably look like an overwhelming confusion of figures, symbols, and shadings. These are really nothing more complicated than a shorthand system, and a complete explanation of all the symbols and their meaning is printed on the back of the map.

Where do boatmen get their weather clues and tips on what kind of weather will be heading their way? They just take a good look at the sky. What kind of clouds are up there? Which way are they moving? What direction is the wind—down on the ground or on the water? How gently or how hard is it blowing? What does the thermometer say? What is the barometer reading? Test the air . . . is it dry or damp? None of these clues means very much by itself, but when you have taken all of these into consideration, you will come up with a fairly accurate forecast.

A bright blue sky usually means fair weather. A vivid red sky at sunset predicts a fair day tomorrow. This same sky at sunrise, however, indicates foul weather that day. Remember the jingle: "Red sky in the morning, sailor take warning," etc.? If the sky is dull and gray at sunset, chances are that tomorrow's weather will be foul. A cloudless sky when the sun goes down is a fair indication of mild and cooler weather tomorrow. You have seen a ring around the moon. That halo is a sure tip-off that a storm is on the way. A weak, washed-out-looking sun indicates probable rain. A diffused and glaring white sky at sunset forecasts a storm coming. A bad night usually follows when the barometer drops and the sun sets in dark clouds. A fair and warmer day is indicated when the ball-of-fire sunset takes place.

When the sun comes up out of a gray horizon there's a good day ahead.

A good boatman is always prepared for the worst. Not all storms that arise are violent; but it is a good idea to assume they will be and prepare for them. Be sure you know the signs of a storm and look for them.

ANCHORING

Where should you drop anchor? There may be a good holding bottom throughout the area you select, or there may be just a few patches of bottom that will give an anchor a chance to hold properly, so try to determine in advance the nature of the waters you are using. Rock bottom and that other extreme, very soft mud, are best avoided. Avoid places where natural underwater obstructions or sunken wreckage may foul an anchor. Keep in mind also that the wind can literally push the water into your anchorage or pull it away —so make sure that you will have enough water to float your boat away. You will want enough of a safety margin so that at low water the boat won't be set down on any projection of the anchor above the bottom. But too great a depth has its disadvantages, too. The more length of chain or line is out, the more work will be involved in hauling it back in.

Once you have selected a spot to anchor, take into consideration the number of boats that may be passing nearby. Be careful not to anchor in the channel or in a busy area. Don't anchor close to another boat, as the wind may very well cause the two to collide. The best way to drop your anchor is to come over the spot you've selected, head into the wind or current, whichever seems to be stronger, stop and lower or drop your anchor. (Needless to say, drop the anchor gently or you may knock a hole in the side of your boat.) Then, as you are carried astern by the wind or current, or by the engine in reverse, begin to pay out scope, gradually putting some strain on the chain or rope. You will soon learn to sense from the pull whether the hook is holding or not.

In setting your anchor, don't try to drag it through the bottom by revving up your engine in reverse. As long as the weather is calm, there is no need to bed your anchor deeply, as breaking it out later will be that much more difficult. Just be sure that the anchor has caught with enough holding power.

It is good seamanship to check your anchor from time to time after it has been down for a bit. The main consideration here is that you should have everything ready for paying out more scope if it should be necessary. It is not a good idea to have two anchors out in a line. The lines may become entangled and prevent giving either of them more scope. Where two anchors are put out, they should be placed so as to allow for a shift in the wind. If one is down and has been given plenty of scope, use the engine to go ahead until well abreast of it, as far off as the line will permit. Then drop your second anchor there and fall back on its line until the boat is bridled to the pair.

Two anchors are often used, angled out ahead to hold the boat in place while fishing. You can accomplish the same thing, however, by making a light line fast to the chain or

rope of the service anchor, having it secured well out from
the bow. Lead the light line outside of everything aft to a
stern cleat. Slack off just a little on the anchor line and/or
adjust the secondary line, and the boat will settle down to
ride steadily.

Hoisting the anchor can be the hardest part of anchoring. This is where good equipment can save you a lot of
time and trouble. A windlass, for example, will permit you to
break the anchor out and hoist it to the point where it can
be lifted up on deck. With a windlass, hoisting can be a
one-man job. If you have a patented anchor hoist or lift, it
is a simple matter to get the anchor up on deck without
scratching the topside or smashing a hole through the boat.
A simple pair of roller chocks will also facilitate getting the
anchor on deck.

If you are having trouble hoisting anchor, take up all
the slack on the line and let it remain taut for a few minutes.
This steady strain on the anchor may loosen it just enough
so that you will be able to hoist it on your second try. The
other way is to use the engine of your boat—edging it forward just enough so that the line will go taut and the anchor
will loosen. Be ready to shift into neutral just as soon as it is
obvious that the anchor has broken loose.

In an extreme case when the anchor is really caught by
some obstruction on the bottom, you will have to worry
the anchor free. Allow just enough line so that when you
move ahead, you will put a strain on the rope. Repeat this
at different angles. Remember, the length of the anchor line
should be at least five times the depth of the water.

KNOTS

Knots are used to join two ropes together or to shorten one rope—and to tie up, tow, haul, hoist, and support objects. The same knot can be used for many purposes—conversely, many knots can be used for a specific job. For example, if you want to secure a mooring line with a firm knot that you can leave at the end of your rope and use many times over, you might use a bowline. However, if you want to moor with a temporary but secure fastening that will untie quickly, you can use any of a number of hitches. Therefore, the purpose of the knot and the conditions under which you will use it should determine the type of knot you will use.

A knot has three parts: (1) The *end* is the end of the rope with which you are working when you tie a knot. (2) The *standing part* is the inactive length of the rope. (3) The *bight* is the central part of the rope between the working end and the standing part.

Following are simple knot terms:

AN OVERHAND LOOP is made by crossing the end of the rope *over* the standing part.

AN UNDERHAND LOOP is made by crossing the end of the rope *under* the standing part.

A *TURN* is taken by looping the rope around an object—or in many cases around another section of the rope itself.

A *ROUND TURN* is taken by looping the rope twice around an object.

Once you have formed a knot, it must be *drawn up*, or tightened, slowly and evenly to make sure that all sections of the knot arrangement keep their place and their shape.

How to Keep Rope Ends from Unraveling

Ragged ends of rope on board a boat mean that the skipper is slipshod and doesn't care about the appearance of his boat. With a minimum of effort you can bind, or whip, the loose ends of a rope so it will be neat and easy to handle. Use a fine yarn, marline or spun yarn, to make the whipping.

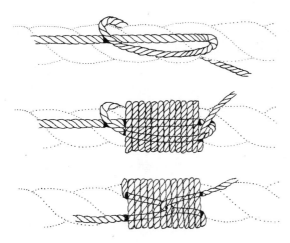

Place the end of the fine yarn at the end of the rope in the form of a loop. Wind the fine yarn tightly around the loop and rope. Wind the yarn to a distance slightly more than the diameter of the rope you are whipping. After winding the yarn, pass the end of the fine yarn through the exposed loop, then pull both ends tight until the loop is hidden. Cut both ends of the exposed yarn short to make a neat finish.

Practice whipping a piece of rope at home. You can use ordinary string instead of fine yarn for practicing.

Useful Knots

Most novice boatmen feel at a loss when it comes to knots because they think they can never possibly know all the knots used by mariners. If you fall into this category, here is something that may console you: very few experienced boatmen are thoroughly familiar with all knots. There are just too many to know and it would take a life-time to learn them all. Most boatmen learn the most important knots that apply to their specific needs, and let the more complicated knots go for others who may need them. Here are a few basic knots that are easy to learn and are useful around boats. You've probably tied them many times without realizing you were tying a knot that has a name.

OVERHAND KNOT. This is the simplest of all knots and is the basis for many other more difficult knots. It is usually used on small-diameter rope because it jams on large-diameter rope and is difficult to untie. Here's the way to tie it: Make an overhand loop. Pass the end under and up through the loop. Draw up tight.

SQUARE KNOT. This knot is commonly used on bundles where two ends of a rope must be joined together. You can undo it very easily by simply pulling on one of the loose ends. To tie it: Pass the left end over and under the right end. Curve what is now the left end toward the right. Cross what is now the right end over and under the left. Draw up tight.

BOWLINE. This knot is widely used for mooring, hitching, lifting, and joining. It never slips or jams if properly tied. It can be tied in the hand or directly around an object. To tie it: Make an overhead loop with the end held toward you. Pass the end of the rope up through the loop, then up behind the standing part, then down through the loop again. Draw up tight.

RUNNING BOWLINE. This knot is used for retrieving objects overboard or for the beginning of bundle tying. It is tied exactly the way a regular bowline is except the end of the rope is passed through the loop where the pole is usually found.

CLOVE HITCH. A hitch differs from a knot in that it is tied directly around an object. Hitches are used for temporary fastenings. The clove hitch is a simple method of fastening a rope around a post, a mooring bitt at the gas dock, or a stake. To tie it, make a turn with the rope around the object and over itself. Take a second turn around the object. Pull the end up under the second turn so it is between the rope and the object. Tighten by pulling both ends.

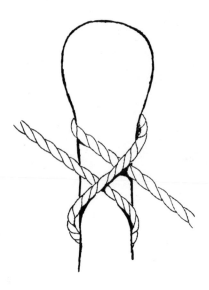

CHAPTER FIVE

Your Trailer

A trailer is an essential part of your boating equipment. Unless you plan to keep your boat permanently docked and never transport it across land, you will find that the boat spends more time on the trailer and in transport than it does on the water—so select your trailer carefully. Even if you dock your boat permanently, you will want to pull it out of the water for checkups and maintenance repairs. A trailer will inevitably be a part of this transportation.

Today, trailers will handle almost every type of boat from a catamaran to a catboat. In recent years boat manufacturers have frequently offered trailers as an integral part of their package, emphasizing the importance of matching boat to trailer.

MATCHING BOAT TO TRAILER

The first consideration in selecting a trailer is the boat it will carry. An improperly matched rig can result in extensive damage to both. If price is a factor, shop around until you find a trailer that will safely handle your boat. You can afford to sacrifice some labor-saving devices if necessary, but make sure the trailer is capable of handling your boat.

Trailers come in three basic styles: The T frame is designed primarily for lightweight runabouts and sells under $150. The A frame, frequently called the box frame, is constructed to carry much heavier boats. The combination T and box frame gives extra support to the stern and hull.

The length of trailer you need is determined by the over-all length of your boat. A 16-foot runabout would require a trailer 16 feet long or longer. It is possible to put a 16-foot boat on a 15½-foot trailer; however, the extra overhang plus the weight of an outboard engine will put an added stress on the boat transom. On a bumpy road you will find that a 125-pound engine extending over the end of your trailer can seriously damage your boat.

The trailer supports should correspond as closely as possible to the hull contour of your boat. A displacement hull, for example, requires a trailer with supports riding at the turn of the bilge, and the keel must be amply supported by numerous rollers. In cases where boats have secondary keels running longitudinally, the rollers or bolsters should make contact with the actual hull and not the keels.

IMPORTANCE OF WEIGHT

WEIGHT CAPACITY. When you purchase your trailer, check to see what weight load the manufacturer recommends for the trailer. If your boat comes within 100 pounds of the maximum capacity, buy the next size larger trailer. Remember, you'll probably be loading the boat down with engine and extra gear.

OVERLOADING. Know how much your boat and trailer weigh. The weight of your boat is important not only when determining how many people you can safely carry; it is also vital to the performance and durability of your trailer. If you know the manufacturer's stated weight of the boat and trailer, add to this the weight of the gear inside the boat and you will know the total weight of your rig. If these statistics are not available, it would pay you to stop at a truck-weighing station along a highway to have your rig weighed.

TRAILER WEIGHT. There are three categories regarding trailer weight: load capacity, net weight, and gross weight. Load capacity is the weight of the boat, motor, and gear. This should not exceed the load limit stated by the trailer manufacturer. Luggage, fishing equipment, or any other extras carried in the boat while traveling should be included in this weight. Place all extra gear in the boat in such a way as to avoid unnecessary stress on any one part of the hull. Make all extra gear secure to avoid shifting or bouncing when in transit. Place the gear above trailer supports. Net weight is the weight of the empty trailer—required by some states for licensing. Gross weight is the weight of the boat, motor, gear, and trailer. This is the load resting on the trailer tires and should be used when checking tire pressure.

TRAILER HITCHES

Make sure that your trailer hitch and ball conform to the current Society of Automotive Engineers (SAE) recommended practice for passenger car trailer couplings. Their recommendations are as follows:

CLASS A: Nonpassenger-carrying utility trailers with a gross weight not to exceed 2,000 pounds. On a ball-type hitch, the minimum diameter of the ball should be 1⅞ inches.

CLASS B: All types, passenger or nonpassenger-carrying trailers, with a gross weight of 2,000 pounds and not to exceed 5,000 pounds. The minimum diameter of the ball should be 2 inches.

CLASS C: All types of trailers with a gross weight of 5,000 pounds and not to exceed 10,000 pounds. The minimum diameter of the ball should be 2⁵⁄₁₆ inches.

If you are carrying an extremely light load you can use a bumper-type hitch for better maneuverability. But for any extensive hauling you should invest in a hitch that attaches directly to the frame or axle of your car.

WINCH MOUNTING

The winch assembly should be mounted in such a way as to meet the recommended standards for bow eyes. If your boat is 16 feet or less, the bow eye should be 16 inches up from the extended keel line of the hull. For boats over 16 feet in length, the bow eye should be 20 inches from the extended keel line. When the boat is being loaded onto the trailer, the winch should lift up on the bow eye. Once the boat is secured on the trailer, the hitch should pull down on the bow eye. The hitch assembly must be securely attached to the tongue of the trailer.

TIE-DOWNS

Make sure that your trailer tie-downs are sturdy enough to hold the boat securely against the rollers or bolsters. Serious damage may result to both the boat and the trailer if the boat separates from the rollers while in transit. Heavy webbing is a good material with which to secure the boat amidship. Chain is the best for the transom tie-downs. Do not tighten the tie-downs too securely as this may be dangerous.

MANEUVERING YOUR TRAILER

It is one thing to get the boat safely rigged on the trailer and then transported to the launching area; it is quite another to get the boat safely in the water. Driving a car with a trailer attached requires know-how. You will want to practice a little before you back into the water with the trailer and its precious cargo. Following are some simple steps in learning to maneuver your car and trailer:

BACKING TO THE RIGHT. Turn the wheels of your automobile to the left when backing up and the trailer will swing to the right.

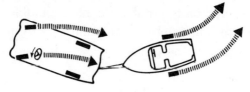

BACKING TO THE LEFT. The opposite procedure is used—when you turn the wheels of your automobile to the right and begin to back up, the trailer swings left.

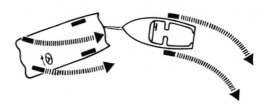

NEGOTIATING CURVES. When approaching a curve in the road, it is of vital importance to remember that the trailer tires will make a shorter arc than the tires of your car. Keep your car as far to the left as safely possible when heading into the curve. With a curve that bears left, keep the car to the right. By taking the curve wide, you will eliminate the chance of having the trailer tires go off the road.

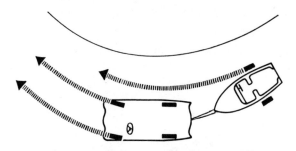

TURNS. This same procedure applies to turns. Swing the car in an extra-wide arc when taking a turn. By doing this, you will avoid hitting the curb with the trailer tire. When entering an intersection, give yourself enough time to safely enter the road in the face of oncoming traffic. An extra-wide turn will prevent you from hitting a car that may be waiting to cross the intersection.

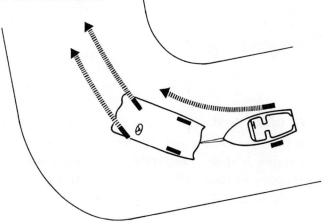

Maneuvering Your Trailer

BACKING YOUR TRAILER. When you back your trailer up to the water's edge, you will most often have to use both right and left turns of the wheel. Once you go into a bend, turn the steering wheel gradually to straighten out the car and trailer into a line. Make sure that as you begin to enter the water, the car and trailer are in an exactly straight line.

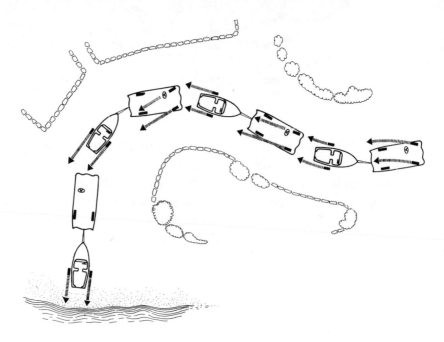

PASSING OTHER CARS. The simple rule about passing other cars on the road is to avoid it whenever possible. Passing with a trailer is quite dangerous; if you must pass, allow yourself plenty of time and room to complete the maneuver.

Gradually pull to the left of the vehicle in front of you, increase speed, then very gradually return to the lane. Most important of all, don't cut the passed vehicle short.

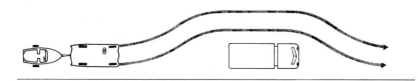

STOPPING. Find out if your trailer is equipped with its own braking system. If it is not, you must be very careful when attempting to stop your rig. The thousand pounds or so pushing your car when you start applying the brakes will greatly increase the stopping distance. You can't stop short with a trailer. Pump the brakes as you come to a stop, allowing plenty of room to make the stop. If your trailer is equipped with its own braking system, use both the trailer brakes and the automobile brakes as you come to a stop. It is a poor idea to use only the trailer brakes when coming to a slow or gradual stop, as it places too much strain on the hitch. Periodically pull off the road when you're en route and check the trailer and the hitch.

LAUNCHING AND RETRIEVING

The spot you select to launch your boat is most important; pick a location that allows an easy launching. A spot with naturally sloping shore, hard enough so the car will have traction, is an ideal site. On sandy or muddy beaches, traction can often be improved by deflating the tires slightly.

There are four basic steps in launching:

1. Back your rig until you are within a few feet of the water's edge. Pull the emergency brake, put the car in gear, and remove all tie-downs. Tilt the outboard engine up and lock it. If you have a tilt-bed trailer, be sure to unlock the tilting device.

2. Release the automobile brakes and back the trailer up until the water reaches the trailer hub caps, providing the water is deep enough to float the boat. Set the brakes of the car and put it into gear.

3. Attach a retaining line to the bow cleat of the boat, unlock the winch, then slowly push the boat off the trailer. Detach the winch line and secure the boat to the shore with a bowline.

4. Return to the trailer and reel in the winch line. Lock the tilt-bed and park the rig away from the launching ramp.

To retrieve your boat, reverse this procedure, making sure the hull rides correctly on the rollers.

TRAILER ACCESSORIES

Trailer accessories are available to help you in difficult launchings. For example, an electric winch that can be detached from the winch stand and installed on the car bumper will pull the trailer through sand or mud. In extreme cases where mud and sand are so soft that you can't back up the trailer, the boat can be unloaded onto air-filled rubber rollers and rolled into the water. A bumper hitch can also be attached to the front bumper of your car to help you maneuver the trailer to the water's edge. This is especially helpful for night launchings, as the headlights of your car make excellent launching lights.

If you are alone when launching the boat, it is a good idea to tie a line to the stern cleat and secure it to a stake driven into the shore line. This will hold the boat against tide or current while you park the car and trailer.

Always carry a length of strong cable in the trunk of your car in case you have to be pulled from a soft beach.

There are many advantages to owning a trailer beside the obvious one of transportation to the docking area. By keeping your boat on a trailer and not permanently docked, you will be able to control to a great degree the weather that the boat is exposed to. You won't have to worry about whether or not your boat is being properly looked after, whether it is being used without your permission, whether it has gone adrift or been run down. You won't have to worry about a terrible storm or hurricane when the boat is safely in your garage.

Another advantage to keeping your boat on a trailer is that when the boat is in your back yard or garage, you can easily repair a loose bow cleat, replace screws, or go over the boat and retouch the paint. Maintenance costs will be much lower because you will find it so convenient to do the work yourself. You will also eliminate storage, shed rent, and wharfage fees. A trailer will soon pay for itself in money saved.

TRAILER MAINTENANCE

Don't neglect the maintenance of your trailer. It can cost you a great deal of money if neglected. Use a wheel bearing grease for the trailer wheels. Anything else you use may possibly result in burned-out wheel bearings. Make sure that the proper air pressure is kept in the tires. An occasional squirt of oil will keep the loading winch in good shape, as well as the rollers and coupling. When launching and retrieving in salt water, try to avoid immersing the wheel bearings.

If you use your trailer in salt water, it is a good practice to hose down the trailer immediately after immersion and wipe it dry.

The usual trailer maintenance jobs are obvious: touch up spots where the paint has worn off; don't let the cradle padding wear down to the point where the boat is sitting on wood or metal; be sure that the gripes (canvas tie-down straps) or lashings are not worn or rotten.

If you keep the boat and trailer in off-season storage, be sure to put blocks under the trailer and keep it off the ground so that the entire weight is not on the trailer wheels. Also, be sure that the boat is supported along the entire length of the keel.

LICENSING YOUR TRAILER

The cost of a license plate for your trailer will vary, depending upon the state in which you live. Check your local authorities. They will also inform you as to the proper placement of the license on the trailer, as this requirement also varies from state to state.

BEFORE YOU SET OUT

Following is a check list. Go over it carefully before you start out with your trailer and boat.

1. Are rollers, bolsters, and other contact points adjusted to the contours of the boat hull?
2. Do the lights, brakes, and license meet the legal requirements of your state?
3. When turned to maximum limit, does any part of the boat or trailer contact the towing vehicle?
4. Do the safety chains allow the proper slack for maximum turns?
5. Is the trailer balanced so that the downward hitch load is within 40 to 125 pounds?
6. Are all moving parts lubricated and operating properly?
7. Are all parts, nuts and bolts, tight?
8. Do you have the correct air pressure in the tires?
9. Are all lights operating properly?
10. Are the boat tie-downs properly secured?
11. Are all safety chains secure? Is the trailer hitch tight?
12. Are the brakes operating correctly?
13. Is the motor tight on the transom and locked or secured in position?
14. Are locks on winch, bunk, or tilt mechanisms in proper position?

15. Check your wheel bearings. Are they properly lubricated?
16. Is your gear and/or baggage evenly distributed, secured and placed over trailer supports?
17. Are your gas tanks tightly closed?

It is highly recommended that gasoline tanks be left empty on long trips and filled upon your arrival at your destination. In case of an accident, the less gasoline spilled around, the better.

OVERLAND CRUISING

There are many ways to make use of a boat trailer in cruising. The most common way is to use the car and trailer to bring the boat to the launching area, and then return at the end of the cruise to retrieve the boat and go home. Another way is to have someone drive the car and empty trailer to your point of destination. This way, you won't have to retrace your steps. The newest and most exciting way to make use of your boat and trailer, however, is in amphibious cruising. This requires quite a lot of planning, but the excitement and comfort make up for all the nights spent over charts.

In amphibious cruising, the car and empty trailer accompany the boat on roads which follow along the chosen waterways on which the boat is traveling. At predetermined points the car meets the boat and crews are exchanged. Most often, the points selected are at the end of a day's run. If your crew can drive a car, it is easy to take turns at this kind of operation. The advantages are many: the car crew can find a good place for a shore meal for everyone at a noon rendezvous. The afternoon car shift can have the responsibility of finding sleeping accommodations for the night. If you plan to camp out, the car shift can locate a camping area.

This kind of overland cruising is especially flexible. It is easy to take off for a movie in town at night . . . you can take side trips to places of historical interest . . . stocking up on food supplies is practically eliminated . . . and the crew gets two kinds of trip at once—overland and overwater!

The other major advantage to amphibious cruising is that it permits you to transport the boat overland where the navigation may be perilous. You can bypass lakes when a storm comes up, you can avoid delay in crowded or out-of-repair locking areas, you can skip the less interesting areas and save time for the areas you do want to see and enjoy. Amphibious cruising is especially well suited for outboard runabouts and cruisers, as it is relatively easy to pull them in and out of the water.

BOATING SEASON

You will find that once you own a trailer, there is no end to the boating season. Winter outboard cruising in the southern states is a lot of fun, and you will think nothing of hitching up the trailer and heading south when the cold winter comes around. You will also be able to explore further . . . going on overland trips to favorite boating spots.

Your trailer is your boat's best friend. Take good care of it, and you'll increase the real enjoyment of owning a boat many, many times.

CHAPTER SIX

Taking Care
of Your Boat

Half the fun of owning a boat is being able to work on it. If tinkering around boats is not your cup of tea, then forget about boating. The enjoyment of painting, scraping, sanding, and scouring is as much a part of boating as the enjoyment of cruising.

Stroll through a boatyard on a warm spring day and you will see avid boatmen toiling on their boats. Many times they are performing painstaking work that would tax the endurance of a professional repairman; yet they work away, enjoying the satisfaction they feel in a job well done. A weekend of working on the boat is one of the most rewarding experiences you will encounter in your career as a boatman.

Fitting out or going into commission are terms applied to the process of preparing your boat for the coming season.

Taking Care of Your Boat

This process is important to your future enjoyment of the boating season and should be planned accordingly. Whether you plan to do a major overhaul on your boat or just get it shipshape for the water, you must approach the work with a definite plan in mind. A systematic approach to fitting out will eliminate duplication and make for a more efficient attack. Of course, the amount of work you will have to do depends on the condition of your boat. Therefore, the first step in fitting out is to determine accurately what has to be done to your boat.

Go over the exterior of the hull with a fine-tooth comb, checking for any rot. Tap the wood with the handle of a screwdriver or ice pick to determine if there is any rot. You will notice a difference in the tapping sound between a rotted section and a good section. If you encounter a rotted section, make a notation on your work sheet. The work sheet can be an ordinary pad on which you note all the work needed to be done.

Be sure to check the wood around a through-hull fitting. This area is usually prone to rot and must be carefully inspected. When you notice a dull sound as you tap with the handle of an ice pick, use the point of the ice pick to probe the wood. If you detect rot, mark the spot with a crayon or colored chalk.

If your boat hull is caulked, check it as you go over the hull for rot. Remember that the planks will have shrunken due to being out of the water and the seams may appear to be hollow. The planks will return to their normal position once the boat is in the water, but the caulking must be pliable. Replace caulking that is hard and brittle.

Once you've completed your inspection of the exterior of the hull, you are ready to inspect the bilge. The bilge must first be cleaned of all traces of oil, grease, and dirt. There are excellent bilge cleaners on the market that are specifically designed for this purpose.

Look for rotten, watersoaked wood. If you encounter dry rot, make a notation to have it remedied. Once dry rot gets into a boat it is hard to stop it. Be sure to inspect every part of the bilge and floor boards, even if it means removing linoleum or other deck covering.

If there is any work to be done, note it on your work sheet. It's surprising how much you can forget if you attempt to keep minor repair needs stored in your mind. The written analysis of your boat's condition is the best record you can have for future repairing.

Even though you have already cleaned the interior of your hull, you will probably have to reclean it after poking around looking for rot or damage. Paint chips and loose wood should be removed from the hull, especially the limber holes (the holes in the frames that permit water to drain to the lowest point of the hull). Limber-hole inspection should be a periodical activity during the boating season. If blocked, they will trap water between the frame members.

TOPSIDES

In an open runabout, topside inspection is just a matter of going over the decks, seats, windshield, and other items with great care. Check for dry rot and damage, making notes on what needs to be repaired. If your boat has a cabin or some type of superstructure, the same procedure should be followed. Naturally, common sense dictates what is necessary to get your boat in shape for the coming season. You don't have to be a professional repairman to recognize a faulty rub rail or a rotten plank. You may not be able to repair it, but you certainly can spot it and bring it to the attention of a person who is capable of correcting the situation.

JOBBING OUT WORK

Again, common sense dictates what work you should attempt yourself and what work you should job out. Major hull work is usually best performed by a seasoned professional boat repairman. Unless you are thoroughly experienced in working with tools and materials, steer clear of any major hull work. If you know as much about boat repairs as the next fellow—but no more—stick to sanding, painting, and minor repairs. You'll save yourself money in the long run because if you attempt to do large-scale repair jobs, it will probably have to be corrected and finished by an expert repairman.

WORK YOU CAN DO

Painting is the field in which the average boat repairman comes to the forefront. With a little patience, he can match the skill of any seasoned refinisher. Of course, the proper paint must be used for each specific application. Here are some tips on painting suggested by a well-known manufacturer of marine finishes.

Painting Procedure

When painting boats, as when painting anything else, you start at the top and work down. The order is: standing spars, cabin exteriors, cabin interiors, decks and deck equipment, topsides, bottom, and boot topping last. If you follow this order, you will avoid the possibility of ruining freshly painted surfaces while working above. This order can be changed if you plan to do some of the painting after the boat is in the water.

Surface Preparation

Slapping paint over blisters, scratches, or a surface that hasn't been properly prepared is a waste of time and money. If the surface looks bad, prepare to take it down to bare wood or metal.

One way to inspect the quality of a surface coating is to give it a few firm strokes with sandpaper. If the finish powders or shows signs of being brittle, it is no longer in shape to do the job it was intended to do. Take it down to bare wood. In the case of metal, rust should be removed with a wire brush or sandpaper. The following rules are for preparation of various boat surfaces:

WOOD. Sandpaper wood to remove imperfections. Be sure that the surface is free of dirt, grease, oil, or any foreign material. Paint only when the surface is thoroughly dry.

Painting Procedure

When working on varnished surfaces, apply new varnish only on old surfaces that insure good adhesion. Remove any questionable finish by scraping, sanding, or by using paint or varnish remover. Remember that the remover may contain wax which will prevent a strong bond between the coating and the surface. Use turpentine or naphtha to remove all traces of the remover.

METAL. Remove both loose or scaling paint and rust by sandpapering or wire brushing. Sandpaper edges of chipped paint to a fine edge so that it will not show when painted. Wash the surface with mineral spirits, kerosene, or washing compound. Be sure the surface is dry before painting.

CANVAS. Be sure new canvas is flat and snug before painting. Clean it of dirt, oil, or grease and paint only when it is thoroughly dry. If old canvas is badly worn or cracked, it is best to replace it. Painted canvas in good condition should be sanded before repainting. The canvas may be in good condition but the paint may be cracking and checking—then the paint can be removed from the canvas with paint and varnish remover. For best results, the area should be liberally wetted with remover, then covered with rags or newspapers. This reduces the evaporation rate of the active agents in the remover. Keep the cover in place for an hour, then remove and scrape the softened paint with a blunt scraper. Take care not to damage the canvas underneath. After the removal operation, brush with a soft wire brush or a stiff bristle brush.

FIBERGLASS. Although most fiberglass reinforced plastic boats have color blended right in with the construction material, there are times when it should be painted. Faded or worn spots should be retouched; or you may want to change the color. It is difficult to get a good bond between plastic and paint, but there are some paints specifically designed for this purpose. If you plan to paint a fiberglass boat, make sure the manufacturer of the paint you plan to use specifically states that the paint will adhere to your type of fiberglass reinforced plastic. There is a wide range of plastics used in boats, and one paint may be excellent for one fiberglass boat, but inferior for another type.

Here are some general rules for applying finishes to fiberglass boats:

The surface should be free of wax, dirt, or grease. Use a detergent or solvent as a washing agent.

A primer coat is usually necessary. It can be applied by brush or spray. Due to the rapid set-up time of most primers, they must be applied to small areas to reduce lapping time. Avoid working in the hot sun or over warm surfaces.

In applying the finished coat, follow the instructions of the manufacturer of the paint, since the application of each product may vary according to the properties it contains.

In preparing the surface of fiberglass reinforced plastic boats for paint, follow the same procedure as for wood, except for using special fillers that will adhere to the plastic. Again, check the manufacturer's recommendations before applying filler compound. Most of them can be sanded like wood fillers.

ALUMINUM. Aluminum is much like fiberglass when it comes to applying finishes—a special primer and finished coat specifically designed for aluminum must be applied. However, before applying the primer it is necessary to etch the hull with phosphoric-acid-based material such as Deoxidine or Metalprep. In the use of these materials, follow the directions of the manufacturer. The use of the etching material will insure good adhesion of the primer to the metal surface. It is important to remember that the etching material should be completely removed by rinsing with clear water before applying the primer. Allow sufficient time for the surface to dry after rinsing and before applying the primer.

Painting Hints

In concluding the painting phase of fitting out, here are some helpful hints:

1. Paint only over dry surfaces and during dry weather.
2. Paint only over surfaces that are clean and free from oil or grease.
3. Apply only as many coats of paint as are really necessary. Follow instructions. Numerous coats of paint, one on top of the other, get so heavy that they break down under their own weight. It is necessary to remove piled-up coats at intervals so as to prepare the proper foundation for new finishes.
4. Brush out each coat thoroughly. Do not apply paint heavily.
5. Stir the paint thoroughly before each application. This means seeing that the pigment is thoroughly mixed in with the liquid portion. Pour part of the

liquid into another can and stir the pigment from the bottom; add the balance of the liquid and then pour from one can to another several times.

6. Wait until the undercoat is thoroughly dry before applying succeeding coats. Allow plenty of drying time for each coat.

7. Paint surfaces frequently enough to prevent decay and deterioration. It is false economy to attempt to save money by not painting when it should be done.

8. Putty all nail and screw holes or apply seam cement after the priming coat has been applied. Attempting to putty these places before putting on the priming coat will result in the absorption of the linseed oil in the putty. This produces crumbling of the putty or seam cement.

9. Use only a first-class primer. The life and durability of a paint coat depend greatly upon the nature of the first coat applied directly to the surface. If the first coat cracks and peels off, so will the finish coats.

10. Do not reduce paint, varnishes, or enamels with linseed oil. It will seriously retard drying, and trouble may result. Follow the label directions.

11. Do not use paint and varnish remover and then follow immediately with a blow torch when removing old paint coatings. Some paint and varnish removers are highly flammable and a surface so treated may catch fire if subjected to a blow torch flame.

12. Varnish only when the temperature is moderately warm (60° or above).
13. Do not shake varnish or enamel. Doing so creates air bubbles which are hard to brush out.
14. Estimate the amount of varnish required for the day's work. Put this amount into a clean can and work from it. Do not put unused amounts back into the original container.
15. Use outside paint only for outside work—inside paint for inside work. This applies except when specifications allow the use of certain paints inside and out.
16. Paint only when the temperature is between 45° and 90°. Cold slows drying time. Hot temperatures are likely to cause blistering or wrinkling.
17. Have plenty of ventilation in the area where you are painting. Some finishing materials have toxic qualities that could cause illness or even death. Never paint in small, unventilated enclosed quarters.

MINOR OUTBOARD MOTOR WORK

During the winter months before the season starts, you will probably have the urge to completely overhaul your outboard engine. If so, curb the urge. Limit your activity to minor maintenance work that does not require the skill of a trained outboard motor mechanic. Even if you consider yourself a fairly competent auto mechanic, do not attempt major overhauling of an outboard engine. The modern outboard motor is assembled with exact tolerances, and bolts and nuts are tightened to exact torque settings. Special tools and knowledge are required to avoid costly damage.

A good spot to start your minor motor work is on the ignition system. Inspect the spark plugs; the use of oil mixed with the gasoline is usually hard on spark plugs. If the plugs are pitted or have a heavy deposit of carbon, they need to be replaced. Be sure to make a periodic check of spark plugs throughout the season, not only for pitting and carbon deposits, but also for the correct gap. The wires leading to the spark plugs should be checked for corrosion. If it exists, take a piece of emery cloth or sandpaper and remove the corrosion, making sure a firm contact exists between the wire and plug. The rubber insulators that protect the spark plugs from corrosion should also be checked for cracks or wear. Put new rubber covers in if the rubber is brittle. This is a condition frequently found in engines that are used in salt water. Moisture can seep in and short out the plugs if the covering is inferior.

The carburetor sediment bowl should also be checked. Even though you can look through the glass of the bowl and see no sediment, remove the bowl and wipe it clean. There may be small quantities of dirt and water that are not visible. The sediment bowl is removed by simply loosening the thumb screw beneath it. Take a look at the gasket between the bowl and the area where the bowl is seated. The bowl doesn't have to be replaced, but it is a good idea to replace the gasket at least once a season. When assembling this filtering system, be sure to seat the sediment bowl in the exact position from which it was removed. The slightest air leak between the bowl and the gasket will result in an engine that coughs and sputters while running.

The only other maintenance work you should attempt on the carburetor is squirting a few drops of thin lubricating oil through the air silencer while the motor is running. Don't attempt to tear the carburetor apart to check the floats or chambers. If you suspect a faulty condition within the carburetor, have an outboard motor mechanic check it.

All fuel lines should be carefully checked during the fitting-out process and during the entire boating season. A broken or damaged fuel line will send a stream of highly explosive gasoline into the bilge of your boat. If the lines show any cracks or leaks, replace them immediately. The rubber fuel lines running from the portable tank to the engine should be kept as short as possible. Coil them on top of the tank so that they will not become entangled with a passenger's foot. This will also eliminate the possibility of loose gear cutting the lines.

Just before you put the boat into the water for the first time, take a soft cloth and put a few drops of fine lubricating oil on it. Wipe the entire engine with the cloth. It won't hurt the paint, and it will go a long way in protecting the hood from weather and water. You can also wax the hood of the outboard engine with automobile wax, just as you would do to your car.

If the blades of the propeller are bent or dented along the edges, install a new prop or have the old one repaired. Small nicks can be removed with a metal file, but seriously damaged propellers should be returned to the manufacturer's representative for factory repairing.

To remove the propeller, you will have to remove the shear pin. This is a simple operation that requires removing the pin that locks the nut on the propeller shaft and loosening the nut. Once the propeller is off the shaft, clean the shaft with steel wool or fine sandpaper. Apply graphite or silicon grease to the shaft and replace the repaired propeller. Tighten the nut and insert a new shear pin. Always carry a supply of shear pins in your tool kit. The purpose of a shear pin is to reduce damage to the propeller if it hits a submerged object. Instead of the object's seriously damaging the propeller, the shear pin shears and the propeller spins freely. Become adept at changing shear pins, because you may have to perform this operation while the boat is in the water and the propeller is jutting over the water in a place difficult to reach.

The battery should be cleaned and the terminals sanded to insure good contact. Have it charged and filled with distilled water.

As one of the final steps in fitting out, carefully go over all moving mechanical parts and give them a good oiling. Do not oil parts that logically do not require oiling, such as nylon pulleys or coated control cables.

In regard to oil, it is important that you know how to mix the right amount of oil with gasoline to lubricate the outboard engine properly. The chart provides an easy method for determining the correct amount of oil necessary to prepare various quantities of lubricated gasoline. When mixing oil with gasoline always pour one half of the gasoline into the tank, then add all the oil. Agitate thoroughly

REFERENCE TABLE FOR PREPARING FUEL-OIL MIXTURES					
GALLONS OF GASOLINE	RECOMMENDED PINTS OF OIL PER GALLON OF GASOLINE				
1	¼	⅓	½	⅔	¾
2	½	⅔	1	1 ⅓	1 ½
3	¾	1	1 ½	2	2 ¼
4	1	1 ⅓	2	2 ⅔	3
5	1 ¼	1 ⅔	2 ½	3 ⅓	3 ¾

before and after adding the rest of the gasoline. Always use fresh fuel and do not prepare more than can be used up in several days' time. It is usually recommended that 50 per cent more than the normal amount of oil be added to the first five gallons of gasoline used in a new motor.

Filling the Gearbox

When filling the gearbox it is recommended that the lower drain plug located at the bottom of the lower unit first be loosened and any water accumulation allowed to drain out. Remove the upper vent plug located on the upper part of the lower unit. A reverse method is used in filling the gearbox. Insert the nozzle of the gear-lubricant container into the lower drain hole and force the lubricant up into the gearbox. This reverse method forces out any water that may be trapped on top of the lubricant. Replace the vent plug and then the drain plug. Make sure the plug gaskets are in good condition, to prevent the entrance of water into the gearbox.

TROUBLE SHOOTING

If your timing is right, you should finish fitting out about the time the boating season begins. After you launch the boat, the first step you will probably take is a shakedown cruise. Use the chart on the next page as a trouble shooting guide during the motor testing phase of the shakedown cruise.

IN-SEASON MAINTENANCE

After you've completed your fitting out and the boat has been launched for the coming season, you will be faced with the pleasant task of keeping your boat in tiptop shape. It's pleasant because one of the appealing aspects of the sport is that you can putter around the boat all season long. Many true boatmen will get as much enjoyment out of going down to the dock and working on their boats as a sea captain gets sailing the high seas.

If you are the type of person who is appalled by good hard work, then steer a wide course around boating. You will be disappointed and the investment you make in a boat

174

Trouble Shooting

IF YOUR TROUBLE IS	CHECK POINT	CHECK POINT	IF YOUR TROUBLE IS
	OUT OF GAS	IMPROPER TYPE OF SPARK PLUGS	
	GAS LINE VALVE CLOSED	CARBURETOR ADJUSTMENT TOO LEAN OR TOO RICH	
	FLOODING	TOO MUCH OR TOO LITTLE OIL IN OIL-FUEL MIXTURE	MOTOR "SLOW DOWN" OR LOSS OF POWER
	INSUFFICIENT PRIMING		
	TOO MUCH OIL IN OIL-FUEL MIXTURE	DIRTY GAS LINES OR CLOGGED SCREENS	
	DIRT, WATER, OR OTHER FOREIGN MATERIAL IN FUEL SUPPLY, CARBURATOR, SCREENS, OR LINES	STUCK RINGS, SCORED CYLINDERS, OR BLOWN GASKETS	
MOTOR MISSES OR FAILS TO START		MOTOR OVERHEATING	
	BROKEN, DISCONNECTED, OR LOOSE WIRING		
	BLOWN GASKETS, IN CRANKCASE, INTAKE VALVES, OR CARBURATOR	SPARK EXCESSIVELY ADVANCED	
		CARBON DEPOSIT IN CYLINDERS	MOTOR "PING"
	FOULED OR IMPROPERLY GAPPED MAGNETO POINTS	OVERHEATED MOTOR	
	FOULED OR IMPROPERLY GAPPED SPARK PLUGS	LOOSE PROPELLER NUT	MOTOR "KNOCK" OR "THUMP"
		LOOSE FLYWHEEL NUT	
	CRACKED OR DIRTY SPARK PLUG INSULATION	WORN CYLINDERS, BEARINGS, OR PISTONS	
	SPARK PLUGS WRONG TYPE OR IMPROPERLY GAPPED	BROKEN PROPELLER SHEAR PIN	MOTOR TURNS, PROPELLER DOESN'T
ROUGH IDLE	WRONG CARBURETOR IDLING ADJUSTMENT	MOTOR NOT DEEP ENOUGH IN WATER	MOTOR RUNS WELL BUT BOAT IS SLUGGISH
	BLOWN GASKET ON INTAKE VALVE	FOULED PROPELLER OR LOWER UNIT	
		DAMAGED PROPELLER BLADES	
	MOTOR NOT PROPERLY CLAMPED TO BOAT	MOTOR NOT DEEP ENOUGH IN WATER	
UNUSUAL MOTOR VIBRATION	CARBURETOR ADJUSTMENT TOO RICH OR TOO LEAN	WORN WATER PUMP	OVERHEATED MOTOR
	FOULED OR DAMAGED PROPELLER	CLOGGED WATER PUMP INLET	
	LOOSE PIVOT BRACKET	BROKEN OR LEAKING WATER LINE	
	NO SPARK IN ONE CYLINDER	TOO LITTLE OIL IN GASOLINE	

will be lost. If you were to ask those rare people who are violently opposed to boating, you would probably find out that they became disillusioned because of the work that is involved. Don't get the idea that boating is all work. Admittedly, it is a large part, but there is still the thrill of having a gleaming hull and glistening brightwork under you as you head out for a cruise. Maintenance and pride of ownership go hand in hand, and one doesn't exist without the other.

The actual amount of maintenance work necessary during the season depends on how much the boat is used. If you use a trailer to get your boat to the launching ramp every time the weather permits, you will have more of a maintenance job. Conversely, minor use requires minor maintenance. But if you have fitted out your boat properly prior to starting the season, the work should be minimal.

As the boating season progresses, you will find out what every boatman has discovered—the season is much too short. Regardless of its length, from three months to nine, it is always a short season to the boatman. And before you know it, it is time for going out of commission.

GOING OUT OF COMMISSION

Most boatmen begin to think about preparing their boats for winter when the winds become cold and the sun no longer gives a comfortable warmth. Others are so caught up with the sport that cold weather just means another kind of boating during the winter months. These winter boatmen have the advantage of uncluttered waterways and cold, crisp days that are perfect for weekend cruising. But to those who desire to mothball their boats for the winter, there is a special procedure to follow.

WHERE TO STORE THE BOAT

The big question is: should you wet or dry store your boat? There are valid arguments for both types of storage. In making your decision, a good rule is to follow the custom of your local boatyard. If most boats like yours are left at a mooring during the winter, then you can feel confident that this method of winter storage will be suitable for your boat. If most boats are dry-docked, then you should seriously consider this method of storage.

Ice, swift currents, and floods are conditions that indicate dry-docking for winter storage. Heavy commercial traffic near the proposed winter mooring is also a factor in deciding on dry storage. Salt water is usually not good for prolonged wet storage. Actually, if your boat is light in weight and requires very little effort to dry-dock it, your best bet is dry-docking for the winter. Of course, if you have caulked seams in the hull that would suffer from drying out and shrinking in dry storage, you would be better off leaving the boat in the water.

The length of time that your boat is going to be stored is also an important factor in determining whether or not to store it on land. If your storage period is only going to be three months, it would be wise to leave the boat in the water. But if it is going to be for six or more months, dry storage would probably be better.

You will also have to consider the cost of storage. Usually, wet storage is less costly than hauling the boat and storing it on land. But price should be a minor consideration when the safety of your boat is involved. Don't keep your boat at a mooring because it is cheaper than dry-docking it. When you are ready to launch the boat, you may find that the few extra dollars you paid were well spent.

When storing the boat on the water, you will have to decide on a mooring or a slip. If tides are a problem or the docking area is unusually rough, then a mooring is your best bet. A protected water slip has its advantages because it permits you to work on the boat and inspect it periodically.

Some type of covering should be provided for your boat. If it is a canvas cover, be sure there is plenty of ventilation without exposing the boat to the elements. A free circulation of air will minimize dry rot and help to keep the boat dry. Make sure the shed is strong enough to hold up under a load of snow or heavy rains if you plan to store the boat indoors. It's surprising how many boats are damaged by falling sheds.

Selecting a Boatyard

If you live in an area where there are very few boats and fewer boatyards to accommodate them, you will have little trouble in selecting a boatyard. But, if you live in the center of a boating community, you will have a problem deciding what boatyard to select.

Where to Store the Boat

Here are some important considerations in selecting a boatyard: It is financially within your means? Have proper fire prevention precautions been taken, such as ample fire extinguishers, sand buckets, or water buckets? Is the yard free of congestion? Many boatyards are so jammed with stored boats that passage of a fire engine or fire-fighting equipment would be impossible. "No Smoking" signs should be posted throughout the yard.

Does the yard have the necessary protection against vandals or trespassers? There should be a guard on duty twenty-four hours of the day for seven days of the week. Yards with high fences around them discourage trespassers. Open yards are too inviting to people bent on picking up some free equipment.

If there is a chance that spring floods might reach a high level in your area, make sure the boatyard you select is high enough to remain dry regardless of the level of flood waters. Check the buildings in the yard to satisfy yourself that they will withstand a heavy snow load or high winds. It is also a good idea to determine how close it is to another yard, since a neighboring fire could possibly sweep over to your boatyard.

If you plan to work on your boat, make sure the yard you select permits owners to work on their boats. On the other hand, if you plan to have the yard men do some of the work, it is wise to select a yard that has skilled craftsmen with a full line of tools.

Once you have selected the yard that satisfies your every need, you can rest assured that your boat is safely dry-docked for the winter.

Of course, you can store your boat in your garage or in your back yard. Many boatmen with trailers will rent an extra garage in which to store their boats. There are even boatmen who have been known to store their boats in the family garage, leaving their automobiles outside during the winter.

YOUR BOAT'S LAY-UP

A number of people will wait until the very last moment, when the snowflakes begin to fall, before deciding on a date to haul the boat out of the water. If you are wise, you will set a haul-out date well in advance, as much as three months. Make arrangements at the boatyard during the height of the boating season, and you will be assured of a storage place.

If you have kept up with preventive maintenance during the season, you will have very little major work to do. Most of it will be a matter of correcting the damage, if any, encountered during the season. There will also be the job of getting the boat ready for winter. As in fitting out, going out of commission should be approached with a definite plan in mind. The four major divisions of a plan for winter lay-up are:

1. Work that has to be done immediately after hauling the boat out of the water.
2. Work necessary to prepare your boat for the long winter ahead.
3. Work that you plan to have done by the professional workmen at the boatyard.

4. Work you can do yourself at your leisure and depending on the weather conditions.

You will probably be tempted to put off doing any of the work until the next season is almost on top of you. Avoid this, because you will be late getting the boat back into the water, and some of the minor work that must be performed immediately after hauling could mushroom into major repair jobs after a long winter lay-up.

The following suggestions will help you to make sure you have taken every precaution to protect your boat during storage.

Hauling Out Your Boat

Even though you have made a date to have your boat hauled out, the yard will probably be so busy that there will be a slight delay. Make sure the boat will be taken care of during this waiting period, and plan to do some preliminary work. Of course, if you are simply going to put the boat on a trailer and haul it to your garage for winter storage, you will not be plagued by these delays. But the same rule of doing the necessary work as soon as possible still applies.

Remove All Gear

Take everything out of the boat that can be easily removed. Stripping your boat will permit more thorough ventilation, simplify work inside it, and keep the weight within the hull to a minimum. Protect your gear by storing it in the house in a dry, safe place. It would be a good idea to remove any equipment that can be repaired at your home workshop or in your living room. Brass fittings or small de-tachable items can be refurbished some cold winter night while you sit before the fireplace.

If you're storing the boat in a yard, here is a warning. When the boat is being hauled out of the water, do not tell the yard man what to do. Chances are he has handled boats much larger or much smaller than yours and he knows what he is doing. You can be present to witness what he does, but do not attempt to give him directions. This is distracting and irritating.

After Hauling

Once the boat is out of the water, make a thorough examination of the hull. If you haven't had the boat out of the water for the entire season, you may discover some dam-age underneath that requires prompt attention.

After completing this inspection, make sure the boat is supported properly. If the boat is being stored in a yard, make sure the shorings are in the correct position to support the vital parts of the hull—keel, stern, and at the turn of the bilge. This same rule applies to boats stored atop trailers. The bunkers of the trailer should support the hull in as many strategic spots as possible. The trailer must also be supported so the tires are off the ground. When blocking up the trailer, make sure the supports are firm and will not topple. If you have enough room in your garage or back yard to store the trailer and boat separately, definitely do so. The weight of the boat resting on the trailer all winter could weaken the springs.

Also keep in mind that you will be working in the boat

while it is dry-docked, so the supports must be sturdy and well placed to keep the boat firm while you move around in it. Another point to remember about supporting the boat on land is not to keep the boat too high off the ground. If the boat should slip, much damage could result; therefore, support the boat as close to the ground as possible. This will also reduce wind resistance if the boat is to be stored outside.

Cleaning the Boat

The first thing to do once the boat is safely in dry dock is to give it a complete wash-down with fresh water and a detergent. If the boat has been used in salt water, washing down is extremely important because marine growth becomes difficult to remove once it dries.

Remove the bilge plugs and let the water drain out. Make sure the drains are not clogged, and once the bilge is drained, give it a good rinsing. After the bilge has been thoroughly cleaned, inspect the hull more closely and record any damage that must be repaired.

Since you have already removed all the gear from the boat, you will be free to move around completely unhampered. If you have left stripping the boat of gear until it has been put in dry dock, make sure you remove everything before completing your final steps in supporting the boat. Hull supports will vary according to the weight of the boat. To make unloading gear easier, put the equipment in boxes. You can mark the boxes for easy identification and store them in a convenient place.

Winterizing Your Gear

Blankets, cushions, mattresses, and other moisture-absorbing items should be thoroughly dried before storing them. Life jackets and buoyant cushions have a tendency to rot if not dried thoroughly; place them in the sun or in a warm room to dry before putting them away for the winter. It's best to hang these items in a dry, warm area. Many safety-conscious boatmen will replace all lifesaving equipment every season. It's not too expensive when it could mean someone's life.

Rope, bumpers, and canvas should be dried before storing and then put in a dry location. Coil the rope on a peg on the wall. Try to store as much equipment off the floor as possible. Hanging storage will permit a circulation of air.

All metal subject to rust and all gear that is oiled during the season should be given a coating of oil. You can use waste crankcase oil or commercial fish oil. Don't slop the oil all over the decks and into the bilge, but apply it thoroughly enough to give a complete coating on exposed metal parts. It's a messy job removing the protective oil coating in the spring, but you will be glad you went to the trouble. Do not oil moving gear that does not need to be oiled during the season. Many nylon pulleys used on the steering cables require no oil. In fact, oiling could ruin them.

Although painting is reserved for spring fitting out, you can do some preliminary work during the winter lay-up. Many foresighted boatmen scrape and sand their boats and apply a first coat of paint. The final coat can be left until the spring.

Metal hardware such as vents, cleats, chocks, and other

fixed equipment should be coated with a noncarbolic vaseline to protect them from tarnishing or rusting. Take the necessary precaution of placing a covering over the coated fitting so the vaseline will not soil other items. In the spring, the vaseline can be removed with kerosene or with a detergent.

If you have a head or sink installed in your boat, make sure the plumbing has been drained of water. Go over the entire boat to make sure there is no water that could freeze and cause damage by expanding.

Winterizing the Motor

More damage can be done to an outboard engine by simply removing it from the boat and storing it in the cellar for the winter than running it for an entire season. A few hours of work will keep it in tiptop shape during the winter. The first step is to wash the engine with a detergent and fresh water. This is especially necessary for engines used in salt water. A few traces of salt in the cooling system will absorb moisture and start rust if left over the winter. A good way to wash out the cooling system is to run the engine in a tank of fresh water for about five minutes. You can add a little detergent or outboard-cooling-system compound to the water, although this is not an absolute must.

Some outboard motors take a flushing plug that permits you to attach a garden hose to the cooling system and flush it out this way instead of using a tank.

After the engine has been thoroughly washed down, drain the gear case by removing the drain plug. Once all the oil and sediment drain out, squirt some kerosene into the gear case and drain. This will flush out any sediment. Fill the gear case with the specified lubricant. Draining the gear case can be left for spring fitting out if you so choose, but if you drain and flush it in the fall, make sure there is a lubricant in it so rust will not set in.

All fuel must be drained from the engine and lines. This is done by removing the fuel lines leading to the tank and letting the engine run out of gas while you are flushing it out in the tank. Remove the drain plug on the carburetor bowl if it has one and rinse the fuel screens in a solvent.

Drain all the fuel out of the fuel tanks and rinse them out with an oil and gasoline mixture that is primarily light oil. This will leave a protective coating on the interior of the tanks. Don't put the gasoline that was left in the tanks at the end of the season into your automobile. Remember the fuel has oil in it and it may damage your automobile engine or make it run inefficiently.

Remove the spark plugs and inspect them. You can replace the plugs during the fall or wait until spring fitting out. Most boatmen prefer to put new plugs in right before the season begins. Regardless of what you do, coat the threads of the spark plugs with grease before replacing them into the cylinder head. Squirt one or two ounces of 30W oil into the spark plug holes. Pull the starter rope very slowly so the oil will coat the cylinder walls. The excess oil will drain out of the exhaust outlet. Replace the plugs after this operation.

Again wash the engine down with fresh water and detergent so the dirt and grime are completely removed. Take an absorbent rag and dip it into a light oil. Wring it out and wipe the entire engine with it. Cover all the exposed parts of the engine with a light film of oil.

The storage place for an outboard engine should be dry and out of the way of daily family traffic. Keep it in your cellar if it is absolutely dry, or store it in your garage. A two-by-four firmly attached to the garage framework makes an ideal motor support. The engine should be stored in an upright position, just as though it were being used. It would even pay you to buy an inexpensive motor stand if you have no place to attach the motor in an upright position. They cost only a few dollars.

Once the engine has been placed firmly in an upright position, cover it with canvas, an old blanket, or any other material that will keep out dust. Plastic cloth is fine, but make sure it's not vinyl, which will stick to some painted surfaces.

Covering the Boat

If your boat is going to be stored outside, make sure the canvas you use is fireproofed. It should be supported in a way that will give adequate ventilation. There is no set rule for proper ventilation except to make sure there is a free flow of air through the boat. The slats you use to support the canvas cover should not be so light that they will not support the added weight of snow. A properly supported canvas cover should not trap any water. Stagnant water will quickly deteriorate the canvas.

If there are days that are sunny and dry, roll back the canvas and let the boat get some fresh air. To make sure you have the proper ventilation, just smell the air under the canvas. If it's musty and damp, you are not getting enough air into the boat.

Once the boat has been fully prepared for the coming winter, don't get the idea that you can sit back and just wait until spring. You should make a point of visiting the boatyard or dry-dock area to give the boat a periodic inspection. After severe weather or abnormal snowfalls, take a look at the boat to make sure it has withstood the punishment. This periodic inspection will set your mind at ease, and assure you that your boat will be ready for another season of cruising.

CHAPTER SEVEN

Enjoying Your Boat

The basic appeal of boating is in its romance and adventure, its thrills and its inherent excitement. It's a sport in itself, and a means to the enjoyment of many other sports. The number of activities available to the boatman is limited only by his own imagination. There's no reason to hop aboard your boat, run it around the lake a few times, and head back for the docks—your boating completed for the day. A little planning can make every boating day more exciting than the day before. Swimming, fishing, water skiing, skin diving, photography, cruising, and games can make your water activities varied and interesting.

SWIMMING

Swimming is, of course, a natural activity for boatmen.

Swimming

It is the rare boatman indeed who doesn't take a good long look at that glistening cool green water on a day when the temperature is way above 90° and just decide to jump over-board and splash around for a little while. Bathing suits are as indispensable a bit of equipment as an auxiliary gasoline tank on those sweltering hot days of summer.

If you are not really an expert swimmer, it's a good idea to wear a life belt in deep water. Currents can be tricky, and what looks like calm, shallow water may actually be quite deep, with a strong undercurrent.

Make sure you select a safe swimming area. If other boats are zipping around at full speed and water skiers come flying by at intervals, it is best to forget about this spot and go on to another, more isolated area. A swimmer can be mighty difficult to spot from a craft skimming along at full speed, so play it safe and give them a wide berth.

When you've selected a spot that is out of the way of boating traffic, anchor your boat firmly. Needless to say, make sure you're not anchored in the channel; even if no boats are on the scene at present, you're asking for trouble if some do come along. It is important to make sure the boat is anchored tightly and will not drift. It can be shocking to find that the boat has moved several yards downstream while you've been splashing around. Always—*but always*—leave at least one person on board the boat. Never go swim-ming alone. The person left on board is an added measure of safety in case of emergency, and also is tremendously valuable as a helper for boarding swimmers. It's pretty diffi-cult to haul yourself aboard a boat, especially from deep water, because when you grab the side of the boat, the lower part of your body has a tendency to curl underneath the hull. Unless a ladder is provided for easy climbing aboard, it's almost impossible to get aboard without help from topside. It is *not* advisable to climb up over the outboard motor.

Don't dive into unfamiliar waters. If you have not swum in the area before, slip over the side into the water. Swim upstream, against the current. If you swim downstream, the current will carry you farther away from the boat than you may suspect, and you will have to swim a long way upstream, against the current, to return to the boat.

FISHING

Fishing is, by far, the most popular water sport. If you are using your boat primarily for fishing, a low-horsepower engine is all that is necessary. A boat is a tremendous asset to a fisherman—it gets him to the fishing area and back quickly and with little effort. All his energy can be devoted to catching fish.

There has been much discussion as to whether or not the noise of an engine will scare away the fish. Some authorities say that fish are frightened by the noise vibrations, while others have conducted tests which seem to prove that fish are oblivious to engine noise. Most of the tests conducted, however, are of necessity confined to a small area; when an outboard is introduced into the water, the fish actually have no place to go to get away from it, so it would seem questionable that the fish are unafraid of the noise.

Tests of this sort are often held with freshwater bass and bluegill fish as specimens. These two fish are particularly insensitive to sound, and therefore do not give a true reaction. Most authorities agree that fish do have some reaction to sound, the degree depending upon the kind of fish. Muskellunge and barracuda, for example, are actually attracted to sound and will attack an outboard motor. The most honest conclusion to be reached is that while some fish are unaffected by noise, others become frightened at certain times under certain conditions, and some will always be badly frightened. Play it safe, and cut your engine long before you cast. Be courteous to other fishermen and do not "buzz" by.

Once you've decided to take your boat fishing, the most important consideration is a good spot to fish. If you're cruising in unfamiliar waters, proceed at your lowest possible speed and scan the water and shore line for possible fishing spots. A gently sloping shore line is often indicative of shallower water, and—especially if weeds are present—is a good spot to try your luck. Watch for sunken logs, shoals, underwater holes, reefs, and sand bars. Even a lily pad can foul up your engine, so steer clear of them. Anchor your boat offshore within easy casting distance. Cast your line in toward the shore and reel it back in slowly, allowing the line to halt briefly at intervals. Most fish, especially the larger varieties, are hesitant about coming out into the open from their protected spots; by allowing your line to pause briefly, you may entice them into darting out and making a quick stab at your bait. For best results, begin your casting with a shallow-running lure and then proceed to deeper-running lure until you make a strike. If, after casting several times at each of the depths in an area, you make no contact with a fish, move on and try your luck somewhere else.

Trolling is an advantageous technique in unfamiliar waters, as it permits the fisherman to cover much more area. Begin to troll offshore where the water is 8 to 10 feet deep. Keep moving your boat at trolling speed into deeper water. If more than one person in the boat is fishing, each should fish at a different depth. This will increase greatly your chances for making a catch. Make wide turns so that the fishing line won't catch in the engine or propeller.

Many of the older engines won't go slowly enough to permit trolling. If this is the case with yours, drag a bucket behind the boat. Needless to say, this technique is effective only in clear, deep water. Shallow or rocky waters will cause the bucket to snag and perhaps even cause some damage to your boat. Plates are available to attach to your propeller which will make a trolling speed possible.

Fishing, like everything else aquatic, has rules, too. Following are some of the more important:

- Cast overhand, not sidearm. You wouldn't want to catch a fellow fisherman in the eye.
- Watch your backcast, and keep your seat when casting. It is very easy to lose your balance and go overboard.
- Keep a look out on the water ahead and traffic in the area when trolling. Even when your total attention is on the business at hand—fishing—keep a part of your concentration on the water around you. Spotting an

oncoming boat in time may save an accident.
• Net your fish with a firm, quick sweep. Don't disturb the boat's balance.

WATER SKIING

More than 500,000 pairs of water skis are sold each year in the United States. Aquatic enthusiasts of all ages—from toddlers to grandparents—have discovered water skiing.

Water skiing is a relatively new sport. The first patent for water skis was awarded to Fred Waller back in 1924. These skis resembled an aquaplane in principal; each one was attached to a rope connected to a bridle, which was pulled by a boat. Another rope was attached to the bow of each ski and then held in the skier's hand. Waller later improved upon this design and came up with what we now know as the water ski. Aquaplaning—riding on a square board which is pulled behind a boat—is actually older than water skiing, appearing about 1917.

The only requirement for water skiing is a boat that can travel at about 20 miles per hour. Even the skis are not an indispensable item of equipment, as barefoot skiing is becoming increasingly popular.

Although the only way to learn to water ski is to get into the water behind a boat with a pair of skis, some basic preparations can be made on land that will aid you by giving a taste of what you might expect to happen when pulled to your feet on skis. While still on land, place your feet in the bindings of the skis and assume the sitting position that you will use in the water. Grasp the handle of the tow rope, keeping your arms straight, and have someone on the other end of the tow rope pull you to your feet. As you rise, keep your legs bent and your arms straight. Make sure you rise quickly and evenly.

With this little rehearsal behind you, you can actually try out the skis in the water. Sit on the back of the skis in about three feet of water, holding the tips above the surface. Tell the boat driver to "hit it" when you are in the correct position and ready to go. Most spills that occur while a skier is trying to rise are caused by his telling the boat driver to "hit it" before he is actually ready to go; so make sure you're relaxed, prepared, and ready to get going before you give the cue. As you rise, keep your legs bent and your arms straight. Don't lean forward—let the boat pull you up. If you attempt to get up yourself, you are heading for a spill. The boat does all the work in getting you up on the skis. You just relax and enjoy the ride; before you know it, you'll be skimming along on top of the water.

The first trick necessary to know is that of cutting across the wake of the boat. Use a short, springlike leap and you'll zip right across the wake. Land squarely on both skis, allowing your legs to absorb the shock.

Making a turn can be a bit trying at first—just lean into the turn as you do when you're riding a bicycle and you'll have no trouble.

Falls are a part of water skiing. In fact, they are the most practical method of stopping. Learn to take the falls gracefully, and no injuries will result. Simply sit down in the

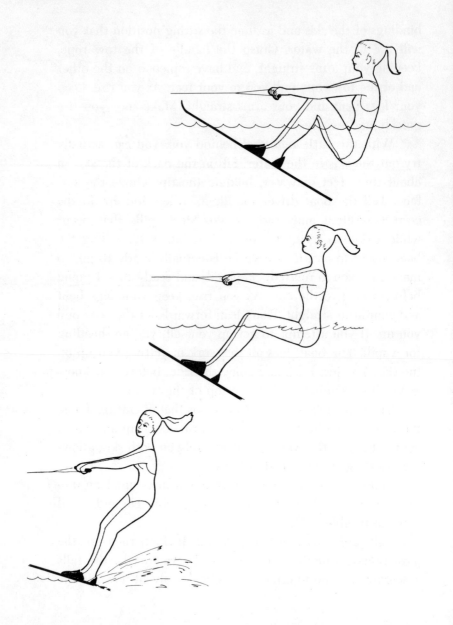

water if you feel you are about to fall. If you fall sideways, curl up into a ball before you hit. Most important, always remember to throw the tow bar clear in order to avoid becoming entangled in the rope.

Surprisingly, it is really not necessary to be an expert swimmer to water ski. In fact, many nonswimmers can be found every day enjoying the fun of skimming across the water on skis. The only really important consideration is a life belt in A-1 condition; this is as necessary for the expert swimmers as for those who sink like a rock. Although life belts and life preservers are not strictly fashionable attire, they may save your life. Even if you are an expert swimmer, a fall while skiing can stun you for an instant, or perhaps you may even get hit on the head by your tow bar or come into contact with floating debris. Even a momentary loss of consciousness could have fatal results if you're not adequately protected by a life preserver. Never—but *never*—go water skiing without that life preserver. Never use last year's preserver without first testing it to ascertain that it is in excellent condition.

Always have at least two people in the tow boat—one to drive and one to observe the skier and tend the tow line. Some states actually *require* that two people must be present in the tow boat. If you're not a good swimmer, make sure that the life jacket you wear will support you easily, and practice just floating in the water with the life jacket so you won't panic if an accident or fall should occur. Always keep an eye on the water ahead of you. Debris can pop up in front of you in the wink of an eye, and only split-second timing and concentration on your path can avert a fall. If you do fall, be sure to hold up a ski or arm to signal the driver you're okay. When landing, come into the shore parallel to the shore and at low speed.

Don't ski in shallow water. A rock sticking up from the water may mean disaster. Be sure of the channel before you ski. Check unknown waters thoroughly before you put on your skis. A sudden shallow area may end your skiing days for a good long time.

Don't wrap the rope around any part of your body. If you should fall, you will want to be free of the boat and not dragged along behind it.

Don't ski at night. You're flirting with danger when you ski in waters where your vision is not clear.

Don't yell "hit it" until the rope is taut and you're ready to take off. A premature yell may send the boat off too soon, and you may get dragged for quite a distance behind the boat.

One good safety hint is to install a wide-angle rear-view mirror in the boat. This will permit the driver to watch the skier behind as well as the waters ahead. Some state laws require this mirror, or a second person in the boat to assist the operator.

Don't tow the skier in heavily traveled or restricted waters such as swimming areas, narrow winding channels, or areas containing docks, floats, and buoys.

When the skier takes a tumble, the boat should approach him from the lee side. Make sure the motor of the boat is stopped before the skier is taken on board. Never start the motor when anyone is in the water near the stern of the boat. When you take the skier on board, be careful not to swamp your boat. In a small boat, it is usually safest to take a person aboard at the stern.

You'll find that a ladder hung over the side of the boat permits the best access.

There are many considerations to safety in water skiing. Five basic factors should be studied:

1. *The water.* Make sure the water is calm enough for skiing. Unless you're really an expert, beware of rough water and high waves.

2. *The boat and motor.* Be sure your boat is built to pull skiers. It must be able to attain a speed of at least 20 miles per hour. Keep your boat in tiptop condition. A good ski boat is light and highly maneuverable. It usually is of a higher horsepower than a comparable fishing or cruising boat. Boats that are open from the front seat to the stern allow an easier and safer access to the ski ropes, motor, and gas tanks.

3. *The equipment.* A coating of wax will help the performance of your water skis. Make sure your tow rope is not rotted or frayed and in danger of breaking. The most important part of your equipment is, of course, your life jacket. Make sure it is in good condition and will support you in the water. Check the label to see if it will hold up your weight in the water.

4. *The driver.* Don't let a "cowboy" driver get to the wheel while you're on skis behind the boat. You need a safe and sane driver. Make sure your driver is

safety-conscious. The driver of a boat towing a skier should realize that he is driving primarily for the skier's enjoyment . . . not his own! The skier should always be the first consideration in any decisions the driver makes.

5. *The skier*. Common sense is the best friend the skier has. Even if you've been waiting for a skiing day for weeks, stay out of the water if the water is too rough, or if visibility is poor. Keep in excellent physical condition. Don't urge the driver to go faster than conditions permit. The highest ordinary speed used in skiing (and this is for barefoot skiing and men's jumping) is 35 miles per hour. Make sure that all of your gear, including foot binders, binder adjustments, and hardware, is as simple as possible and is free from sharp or protruding surfaces that could scrape or cut the skin. Loose runners or binders are not only dangerous but they will impair your skiing efficiency. Several skiers skiing together with ropes of different lengths is frowned upon as a bad practice. If the skier on the long rope should fall, there is a chance that his rope will wrap around the other skiers.

Skiing is fun. You're sure to become so engrossed in this exciting sport that you'll want to go water skiing all day long. It is important, however, to remember not to overdo it. Too many hours on the skis can cause fatigue; not only will you cease to learn to become a better skier, but you will become a hazard to yourself and to others. When you're tired, get off the skis!

Water Skiing Signals

Needless to say, when skiing across the open water with the wind in your ears and the noise of the motor resounding across the open water, vocal communication between the skier and the driver of the boat is impossible. The American Water Ski Association has developed a series of signals to use as a method of communication between the skier and his pilot or observer.

To signal a jump, raise your hand sharply, palm down, and imitate a jump.

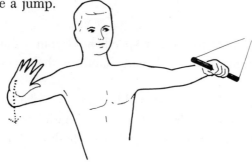

A turn is signaled by a vertical palm and a curving motion with the hand in the direction desired.

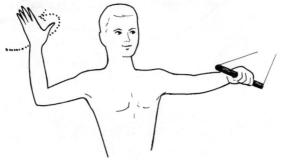

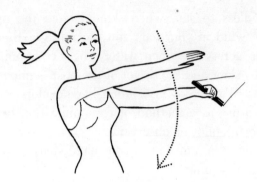

To signal for slower speed, hold your palm down and motion downward with your hand, or shake your head signaling No.

For a faster speed, hold palm up and make a motion upward with your hand. If you need both hands on the rope, a faster speed may be signaled by nodding your head Yes.

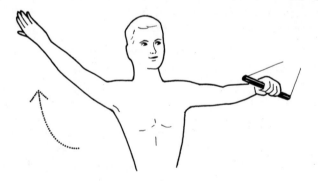

If the speed is okay and you want the driver to know that you are happy with it, make an O with your thumb and forefinger.

To whip off, point to the direction and then give quick circular motions with your hand.

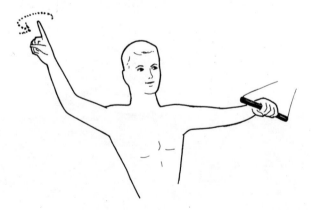

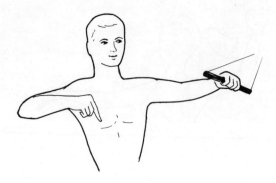

When you wish to return to the dock, extend your arm and bend your elbow so as to point downward with the fore-finger. Straighten your arm sharply, bring the forefinger and arms smartly into a downward pointing position.

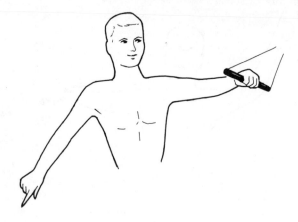

To stop, signal the driver by holding your hand up, fingers outstretched, much like a policeman does.

To signal the driver to cut his motor, draw your finger sharply across your windpipe in a cutting motion.

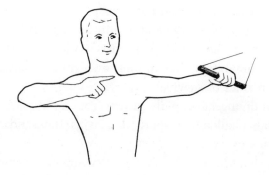

Water Ski Clubs

The increased activity in water skiing has prompted the formation of clubs devoted strictly to furthering water skiing as a sport. If such a club exists in your area, make a point of joining it. Almost every water ski club holds some type of activity on holidays and weekends. Many of them supply the entertainment for boating events. Write to the American Water Ski Association, Lake May, Winter Haven, Florida, for the name and address of the water ski club nearest you. If there is not an organization in your area, the AWSA will tell you how you can form one.

SKIN DIVING

Once you are out in your boat and used to enjoying the thrills and excitement atop the water, your curiosity will naturally lead you to find out what's down underneath that sea of mystery. Nothing can be quite as beautiful or quite as fascinating as the world that exists underneath the water. Here, the inhabitants live in their own rhythm, according to their own rules of survival.

Skin diving has rapidly grown from an obscure pastime to a vital, challenging sport that wins thousands of new aficionados every year.

You don't have to be an expert swimmer in order to skin dive. The best skin divers are those that feel at home in the water, those that do not panic easily, those that can think and act quickly in an unfamiliar environment. When a diver leaves his familiar twentieth-century world and enters that prehistoric fight for survival among underwater plants and creatures, he must meet them on their own level. He is, in a sense, stripping himself of all the technical advances man has made, and is meeting this new and exciting—and at the same time centuries-old—world on its own terms.

The first requisite for skin diving is that the diver be in excellent health. Most important, his nasal passages must be clear and free from sinus problems. Heart and lungs must be in top condition. A great deal of pressure is exerted on the human body when it is many feet below the surface of the water, and it must be able to meet this additional burden. Hypertension, allergy to cold, or eye defects are serious enough to keep you *above* water. If you are a diabetic—even if you receive treatment through injection or by mouth —do not skin dive. If you have a facial deformity that prohibits the mask from setting properly on your face, play it safe and do your swimming above water.

Although you don't have to be a Tarzan as a swimmer, you should be able to swim at least 1,000 feet, tread water for about a half hour, dive about 10 feet into the water and swim underwater for about 50 feet.

In skin diving, the "buddy system" is always essential. Never, under any circumstances, go skin diving alone. You are flirting with tragedy if you do.

Basic Equipment

Although you can go skin diving by taking a deep breath, flipping over the side of the boat, and swimming underwater, the use of proper equipment makes skin diving more exciting. The equipment you use will enable you to stay under water for long periods of time; it will make visibility more clear; it will keep you warm and comfortable. Most important of all, you will be safer with diving accessories. Study carefully the following items of diving equipment and their functions; select from them the diving aids you will need.

THE MASK. The most important function of the diving mask is to enable the diver to see clearly under water. It also performs the secondary function of forcing the diver to breathe through his mouth. No air enters the nose through the mask and the diver must breathe—as divers should—through the mouth.

In selecting a mask, first consider its shape. Be sure that the mask fits your face properly. An oval-shaped mask is usually the best fit for the average face. Proper fit is necessary to permit a good seal against the water, and for comfort over a long period of time. Select your mask by placing it over your face without strapping it to your head. Inhale. If the mask sticks to your face by suction, you can be sure that it fits your face. Next, put the strap in place and inhale again. If in both tests no air leak is detected, you can be reasonably sure that the mask will fit in the water. In order to check for comfort, make sure that the mask edge just under your nose does not rub or push against the wrong spot. If it does, you will feel the strain even when worn for a short period.

If your eyesight is impaired, special lenses can be

ground to your prescription and fitted into your diving mask. The cost will vary according to the complexity of the lenses and the final shape of the mask.

FINS. Fins increase the efficiency of the diver, enabling him to swim with greater ease. Extra motion in kicking just wastes the diver's energy and his air supply. There are two basic types of foot fins available: the first uses a straight reinforced blade with a pocket for the foot and a strap to hold the fin to the heel; the second uses a blade that is set off from the foot pocket at an angle which makes it almost horizontal when it is in the water, but leaves the foot in its normally relaxed position. Once you are experienced in the use of fins, you will find that a long fin with a large blade will give you the best performance.

Consider comfort first in the selection of your swim fins. A powerful, stiff fin is useless if it feels uncomfortable and cumbersome. The open toe, offset-blade fin is probably the most comfortable fin for the beginning diver. The fit is usually better and, as the heel is not strapped in tightly, there is less of a tendency to ankle cramps. Open-toe construction also fits the foot more comfortably, as there are fewer fin sizes than shoe sizes, and it eliminates contact with the foot pocket.

Before buying fins, try them on. Even better, try them out. If possible give the fins a real water test before purchasing them. Some fins float and some sink. Floating fins are usually a little more expensive. If you select fins with adjustable heel straps, be sure that replacement straps are available in case of breakage.

WEIGHT BELTS. The function of the weight belt is to help the diver overcome his natural tendency to float. In order to determine the correct weight necessary to help you stay under water, you must use a trial and error method. Get into the water with full equipment and a full tank of air. Add weight to your belt until you reach a point where on a full breath you tend to float, and on a small inhalation you sink. Because, as you breathe air from your tank, you will be progressively lighter in the water, it is a good idea to add just a pound or two for compensation.

If you are using a dry rubber suit, however, you will have to add the minimum amount of weight and then add more as it is necessary. The air spaces in a dry rubber suit will be compressed by water pressure and you will find an increase in density. Therefore, with this dry rubber suit, remember to start light and add only the weight that is absolutely needed. For the novice diver, it is better to be too light than too heavy.

The belt section of the weight belt deserves special consideration. Make sure that it is fastened with a quick-release buckle. In case of emergency, you will want to be able to jettison the weight belt quickly. One word of warning: do not use a surplus cartridge belt as a weight belt. The buckles on these belts are not the quick-release type, and if your hands are cold or injured, or if you are just plain nervous, you will find it almost impossible to open them quickly. On the other hand, this belt may open by itself at any moment, and you may find yourself suddenly ascending. Put your weight belt on last. It must be worn over all other clothing. Do not fasten any flotation devices to your weight belt; you wouldn't want to lose them if you needed to drop your belt.

SNORKELS. A snorkel is a device that enables you to breathe under water. It is usually 12 inches long, and permits breathing just under the surface of water. Using a snorkel is work, and after a day of snorkeling you will be completely exhausted physically. A snorkel is not a substitute for an aqualung. You cannot dive down 10 or 12 feet or deeper and expect to use a hose to breathe through; the physical exertion of pulling the air down that far is an impossibility.

Snorkels come in many shapes and sizes, and employ several different types of valve. The best way to find the correct snorkel for you is to go and see them all and try them out. Durability is an important consideration in a snorkel, and the rubber snorkel is almost indestructible.

DEPTH INDICATOR. You will probably find that you will use your depth indicator most often for its ability to tell you the maximum depth obtained or the depth to a given spot. Professional divers, however, use the depth indicator as an indication for decompression.

You will need a depth indicator if you dive to a greater depth than 36 feet, or if you use more than one 70-cubic-foot cylinder of air in a twelve-hour period. If you are not sure how long you will be under water, be sure to carry a good watch and a submersible decompression table. Remember, when purchasing a depth indicator, you get what you pay for. A good indicator does not necessarily cost a fortune, but be sure to get one that is of a good quality and reliable, even if it costs a few cents more. Your life is worth it.

FLOTATION DEVICES. Self-rescue flotation devices are carried directly on the diver, while surface-floating types are pushed or towed on the surface. The self-rescue types are usually folded into a small packet and inflated by means of a small carbon dioxide cylinder. The diver simply squeezes the packet and it inflates. Many divers use the familiar "Mae West" life jackets—these are very practical. Some divers use an inner tube or an air mattress as a flotation device. These provide ideal resting places between dives. Bright colors are recommended, as they can easily be seen from a distance. A diver's down flag must be used to indicate to passing boats that a diver is below. The flag is an orange-red one with a diagonal white strip. Red flags are discouraged because they are often confused with storm warning flags.

Inflatable life preservers do not zoom you to the surface like an elevator. They float you to the surface easily and slowly.

KNIVES. A knife will enable you to free yourself from fish lines, nets, or weeds. You may purchase special buoyant knives that will float to the surface if they slip from your hand. You will probably find that a double-edged blade fits your needs best, as you won't have to check constantly to see that you are holding the knife properly.

Select a double-edged-blade with one smooth and one saw-type blade. The saw-type blade will cut almost anything, and you will probably use it even more than the smooth blade. Make sure that you have a sheath for your knife. It is extremely dangerous to dive without a properly guarded knife. Stainless steel sheaths will rust a little, but they can be cleaned up with a little patience and elbow grease. Plastic sheaths bend easily and it's not impossible to jam the knife right through the sheath and into your leg. Fiberglass sheaths are excellent.

Always carry a knife with you on your diving expeditions. You never know when you may have to use it. Although it is extremely unlikely that you'll have a battle with a shark, or become greatly entangled in underwater growth, it could happen. So be prepared for all eventualities—carry a knife.

FLASHLIGHT. On a bright day, when the sun penetrates deeply into the water and a light bottom helps to reflect the light, you will not need a flashlight. However, when skin diving in caves or darkened areas, or where the bottom is dark-colored, you will find a flashlight very necessary. In dirty water, a flashlight is useless; the dirt particles simply reflect the light back in your face. You can buy a commercial underwater flashlight, or you can easily rig one of your own by simply turning on a flashlight and putting it in a mason jar and sealing the cap. Your battery won't last long, but it will serve the purpose.

GOGGLES AND EAR PLUGS. Goggles are an unnecessary part of skin-diving gear. They are even a detriment to safe diving, as they distort and play optical tricks with underwater vision. Ear plugs are just plain dangerous. Never under any circumstances use ear plugs with Scuba gear. Air may be trapped in the passage from the eardrum to the outside; when pressure is applied, the trapped air is compressed as the eardrum bends outward and the ear plug is pushed in by water pressure. Surgery might be necessary to remove the plug. The eardrum may rupture if it is permitted to stretch too far in either direction. Never seal the outer ear with anything when diving.

DIVING LUNGS. The purpose of a diving lung is to permit you to breathe under water. It does this by forcing pure air into a cylinder strapped on the diver's back. A regulating system permits the air to pass from the cylinder to the diver's mouth through a breathing tube. When the diver inhales through the mouthpiece, he is drawing the air from the cylinder through a regulator. When he exhales through the mouthpiece, the used air is channeled through the exhaust tube and out through the water.

There are many types of diving equipment. Before buying a diving lung, read all the literature supplied with the various brands of lungs and make sure that the one you select will fulfill all the functions you demand of it. Don't try to cut corners on your diving lung—it's probably the most important part of your diving equipment. Your life will depend on it.

Once you are satisfied with all the safety features of the lung you select, make sure it fits comfortably. You will be using this lung for many hours, and an uncomfortable diving lung can turn hours of enjoyment into hours of underwater agony. A spot that rubs or presses can become torture. If you can rent the type of equipment that you intend to buy, take advantage of this. It will be a good chance to water-test your equipment fully—and the only way you can tell about equipment is actually to use it.

Do-it-yourselfers have made inroads into the diving-lung field. Many a diver began his careers with a converted Air Force diluter regulator. However, of all deaths caused by equipment failures, home-built lungs account for the highest number. In the hands of a novice, home-built lungs are a time bomb that may go off at any moment. Unless you are a tremendously experienced diver with years of know-how and the courage of a lion, stay away from them. Many good diving lungs can be bought in almost every price range. Your lung is your lifeline . . . don't skimp on it.

DIVING SUITS. You can go skin diving without a diving suit. In tropical or warm waters, such a suit is often unnecessary. But when diving in cold water or to great depths, a suit is a necessary protection against the cold. It is also a protection against dirty water. The diving suit as it is used today consists of two basic designs: the dry suit and the wet suit.

The dry suit is usually made up of an outer garment made of sheet or foam rubber. It covers the entire body and the head. The face and the hands are the only parts of the body that come into direct contact with the water. In very cold water, the hands are also covered. Dry suits are available in front-entry, neck-entry, and waist-entry designs.

The wet suit consists of a blouse, pants, hood, and boots, all of which are usually made from foam neoprene. The suit is not watertight at the points where the arms and legs are exposed, and it is used in waters that maintain a temperature above 55° F. A wet suit is very similar to a dry suit in appearance. The difference is that the wet suit admits water around the neck, wrists, ankles, waist, and zipper seal. Once the water is admitted, it does not flow through the suit, but is trapped and then warmed up by the body heat. The most important factor about a wet suit is its fit; it must fit well in order to function properly. A sloppy fit will allow water to circulate outside and inside and will destroy the warming effect. Wet suits can be worn underneath dry suits for water lower than 55° F. in temperature.

The most important thing to remember about skin diving is *never go alone*—the "buddy system" is never more vital. Don't dive headfirst from the boat with your diving equipment; the lung may hit the back of your head and knock you unconscious. Sit on the edge of the boat and flip over backwards, allowing your lung to hit the water ahead of you. Needless to say, be sure that the engine of the boat is turned off. Stay away from the propellers. Have one man in the boat constantly, and dive in pairs. Mark the area in which you are diving with a flag, so that passing boat traffic will be aware that a diver is in the area.

Skin diving is a highly specialized sport. Anyone who plans to try it should first get as much professional advice as possible.

PHOTOGRAPHY

Photography has a special place in boating. You will find that a camera will probably be the companion that most often goes with you on all your boating activities. A

35-mm camera is especially convenient on outings, as it is small, easy to handle, and can be held firmly. Since the motion of the boat makes photography difficult, it is best to have a small camera that can be braced to minimize all movements. Keep your camera in a place where it will not be in danger of slipping overboard. Remember that when taking photos across the water, the intensity of the sun is magnified; you must close the shutter of the camera so that only the light you need is admitted. With some exceptions, photography on boats is much the same as photography on land. Use the same rules of composition, interest of subject, and correct exposures that you would on land.

Underwater Photography

It won't be long after your first skin-diving experience that you will be bitten by the underwater photography bug. The secrets beneath the water are aching for expression through your camera. You will want to share your fascination with others not lucky enough to be able to see them for themselves. Underwater photography has come into its own as an independent hobby as well as an important phase of skin diving. You can use almost any kind of standard camera for underwater photography if you equip it with a protective box to seal out all the water. The camera case is a very basic consideration, as it must provide watertight protection for the camera as well as enable the diver to manipulate all of the controls of the camera from the outside.

Selecting an Underwater Camera

It is not impossible to lose a camera underwater. You

may at some time or other have to jettison the camera and surface quickly. With this in mind, it is wise to select a camera in a price range where you won't be tempted to endanger your life by trying to hang on to it in an emergency. Another consideration is that regardless of the amount of money you pay, the case might leak or become damaged, and the camera will be ruined. A 35-mm camera is a good choice for underwater photography as it will carry more film per loading than other standard still cameras. Try to select one that contains push-type or revolving-type controls. It will be much simpler to operate these controls from outside your case. A synchronized flash will help you with lighting problems when the bottom is dark.

If your camera gets wet in fresh water, dry it out. It will probably function as well as when it was new. In salt water, however, a wet camera is a ruined camera, so make sure the protective case is of first quality.

Taking good underwater pictures requires patience and much trial-and-error experimentation. The light-filtering effect of the water can change very rapidly—for example, only about 5 per cent of the light may be lost by reflection when the water is calm, but a ripple or small wave may cause this to go up to about 20 or 30 per cent. Color photography is a special challenge, as 15 feet of water filters out reds and yellows almost completely unless artificial light is used.

Don't be afraid to try. The only way you will become a good underwater photographer is to take pictures—plenty of them.

CRUISING

Cruising is one activity that can be enjoyed by your whole family, by your friends, and by other boatmen—all at the same time. You may cruise with a few members of your own family or friends, or you may decide to team up with a whole fleet of boating enthusiasts and go off on a group cruise. No matter which you prefer, you will find that the fun is unequaled. It will permit you to engage in other water sports enroute. You can stop to swim, water ski, skin dive, fish, and enjoy all the pleasures of boating.

A cruise, however, is more than just hopping aboard and heading out for points unknown. It is like a vacation—long dreamed of, long planned for, and long enjoyed. A cruise can be an overnight jaunt, or a tour lasting a month (or several months). The important thing is to plan for it and solve problems before they occur.

YOUR BOAT. The first consideration in cruising is your boat. What type of boat do you have? Will it be comfortable for extended cruising, or should you limit your activities to occasional overnight trips with a few athletic outdoor people? If your boat does not sleep several people comfortably, it is not a good idea to try to travel for days or weeks at a time. Even the greatest boating buff will tire pretty quickly when his creature comforts—such as a good night's sleep—are infringed upon. There are many things you can do to improve the comfort aboard your boat, but the basic room must be there.

Where do you plan to cruise? If you own a small, flat-bottomed boat, you will stay away from offshore or rough waters. You must take into consideration the limitations of your craft. A boat that is perfectly safe in your local waters may be unbelievably dangerous when pushed beyond its capacity. Select your cruising area according to the boat you will be using.

TIME. How much time do you have available for your cruise? If you plan to cruise several hundred miles and enjoy fishing at a particular spot and then cruise the several hundred miles back, you had better have more than a week or so at your disposal. Plan your time so that if you have a destination in mind, you will reach it and be able to enjoy it without having to push back immediately.

You must plan your cruise so that you will know approximately how far along you will be at any given moment. A cruiser can usually average 50 miles a day, but (and this is an important "but") rough waters, bad weather, locking through, stops for swimming, lunch, and many other obstacles to speed will play havoc with any time schedule that requires 50 miles per day. It is much better to cover less distance and permit time to stop and sight-see, swim, picnic, and allow for delays at locks. Plan your cruise so that you can enjoy every moment of it leisurely.

Check the weather before you set out. If storm warnings or bad weather reports are out, perhaps you may decide to stay in port for that day. Don't let bad weather surprise you if you can possibly help it. Your boat may not be equipped to handle the really rough weather that creeps up in many sections of the eastern part of the country. Make sure that your timetable permits time out for it.

Long before you jump aboard and shove off, obtain complete charts of the area that your trip will cover. Mark the spots where you plan to spend the night. Check the areas to see if overnight accommodations and dockage facilities are available. If you plan to camp out, make sure that the spot you pick isn't private property. You may be asked to leave, or worse, be charged with trespassing. Check the areas in which you can replenish your supplies. If a little town or village is marked, it's possible that you will be able to stock up on food and gasoline. Be sure to check your entire proposed route for locks or particularly bad spots in the water.

Plan time out during the day for activities. If there is a spot of historical interest in the area, dock for an afternoon and look it over. A movie in the evening can be quite a morale booster, so plan to spend some nights in areas where you can walk up into town and see one. Some marinas and yacht basins have shower facilities; try to locate them— you will find them welcome.

The Ship's Log

Prepare to keep a log of your cruise. You can purchase regular log paper at your marine dealer's or nautical supply store. Then write in the log every day, giving details of your cruise—what happened, the course at which you are traveling, the amount of gasoline you are using, the speed at which you are going, how the stores are holding out, and all the incidents of your trip. This log will be useful in two ways. First, in the event of an accident the log often will be legal and admissible evidence in any court of law should questions arise. Also, as the log gives detailed descriptions of your trip, you will be able to compare this particular voyage with later cruises over the same or comparable areas. It is most important to remember to sign your log book every day. The only thing that really makes the log book legal is your signature. Keep the log wrapped in neoprene or oiled silk to protect it from water and spray. Write in waterproof ink so that if the log does get dunked in the water it will still be readable.

Duties of Crew Members

Before setting out on your cruise, assign duties to all members of the crew. If everyone knows what his specific job is right in the beginning, it is easier to get him to co-operate and it stalls off arguments later. Appoint a galley slave (cook) and a navigation expert. Try to arrange a schedule whereby, if everyone sticks to it, all duties will be completed with the least fuss possible, and everyone will be able to have more time to enjoy the cruise.

What Do We Eat?

Meals aboard your boat can be a pleasant and delicious part of your cruise. They take careful planning, and on an extended cruise you will undoubtedly want to break the monotony of eating aboard by an occasional dinner in town.

The first consideration in planning meals for a cruise is the number of burners you have available. A cruiser usually has two burners, or facilities for cooking two items at the same time. If this is the case with your boat, you must take care not to plan more than two cooked foods to be eaten at the same time. One way to get around this limitation is to include items in your menu that can be cooked together . . . for example, tomato sauce, rice, and meat balls. One-dish main courses are the best on a cruise. They are easy to prepare and easily served. They also usually require less storage space. Have desserts you don't have to cook.

Consider also the amount of refrigeration space you have available. You will find that some refrigeration is absolutely necessary, so if you do not have a small refrigerator aboard, make do with a Scotch cooler or other ice-box substitute. Hard-boiled eggs previously prepared at home will be a welcome addition to your food stores. They are useful as parts of a main dish, as a salad, or in sandwiches. You will also find many uses for meat loaf prepared at home. You probably have no oven aboard, so don't bring anything that needs to be baked.

Basic menu items suggested for your cruise are:

Ice (useful in drinks)
Water (keep a large container of drinking water aboard)

BREAKFAST: Coffee, tea, milk, cream
Hot and/or cold cereals
Eggs, bacon and/or sausage
Bread, butter
Marmalade, jam
Juices
Fruits in season

LUNCH: Sandwich fillings, spreads
Canned fruits to be eaten cold
Canned salmon, tuna, chicken, sardines, to be eaten cold
Mayonnaise, mustard, ketchup, peanut butter
Tomatoes, lettuce
Pies (don't stock too many as they may spoil)
Soft drinks

DINNER: Crackers and cookies
Canned soups
Canned meat
Potatoes, either canned or fresh
Vegetables
Applesauce
Puddings and mixes

Do not throw leftovers overboard. Keep the garbage in a box or bag and dispose of it in the proper receptacles on shore. Keep the waterways free from garbage. Keep the beach free from clutter, too. You may want to picnic again later in this same area—or another boat may stop here in a few hours. A box or sack on board to collect rubbish in will solve the problem nicely.

The Galley

A properly equipped galley is the key to meals aboard. You will find that if you keep your galley clean and your pots and pans shining, and have a well-stocked cupboard of food, meals on board will be a pleasure. A galley should be equipped with the following:

Stove
Fuel, matches
Two saucepans
One frying pan
Knives, forks, and spoons (stainless steel or plastic)
Serving spoons (stainless steel or plastic)
Griddle-cake turner
Dish mop, towels, steel wool, paper towels
Food containers
Water jar
Coffee pot
Detergent and soap
Plastic or paper dishware

Cleanliness Aboard

It is essential to keep your boat clean. One of the best helps to a neat and attractive boat is proper storage space. If your boat is not equipped with cupboards or shelves for storing utensils and supplies, it is well worth the time and effort to put in a few shelves or nooks. Keep a list of all stores on board and key it so that you can tell exactly where they are kept; it will save time. It will also be a great aid in telling you when you must replenish your supplies.

Hints on Boat Care When Cruising

1. Use detergents to clean your boat.
2. Clean the windows by washing them with vinegar and water before soaping them. This will cut the grease and make them sparkle. Clean the windows

with paper towels rather than with a dishcloth.
3. Bilges can be made to smell sweet by using just a bit of essence of spearmint.
4. Use ammonia as a grease cutter when cleaning your boat.
5. Coffee grounds put into a greasy pan will absorb the grease and make cleaning all the easier.
6. Lemon oil makes mahogany shine.
7. Clean up messes as they happen—when dirt accumulates it becomes more difficult to clean thoroughly. If you look after the boat constantly, you will find that cleaning is not too much of a chore.

Insects

Uninvited guests appear on every cruise, for as long as you are on the water or in relatively uninhabited areas, you will find insects. Take along spray cans of DDT or other insecticide. If you plan to sleep on board, it is a wise precaution to carry mosquito netting. Special lotion can be purchased that, when rubbed on the body, will repel mosquitos. The best attitude to take toward insects is one of inevitable coexistence. You will never be free of them, so learn to get along. Keep your boat spotlessly clean and be sure to get rid of all food remains promptly, and you will help to reduce the insect menace.

Money

It is unwise to carry a large amount of money on a cruise; it may be lost overboard in one way or another.

Also, on a cruise you will want to enjoy yourself and not worry about a huge cache of money hidden in the boat. One of the best solutions is to use traveler's checks. These are easily cashed, and require no identification other than your signature in the presence of the cashier.

Mail

If you are planning to be away for quite some time, you will want to make provision for receiving mail. One of the best ways to arrange for your mail is to have it sent in care of a mail port maintained in co-operation with the major oil companies. Contact your local oil company and inquire if they have this service. Another way to receive mail is to have it sent in care of a marina or yacht club at which you will be staying overnight. In this case, it is necessary to plan your trip well, so that you actually stop overnight where you say you will. Another way to receive mail is, of course, in care of General Delivery in the towns near which you will be passing.

Clothing

Take enough clothes so that you won't be forever doing laundry, but don't load down the boat with excess clothing either. A basic list of clothing for your cruise should include shirts, slacks, shorts, sneakers, boots, jackets and sweaters, underwear, socks, nightwear, handkerchiefs, rainwear, bathing suits, and caps. Consider all the ranges of temperature when you get your clothes together. Remember, that although the days are hot, the nights can be pretty cool, if not downright cold, along the water. Be sure to take along some warm clothing for protection against cool mornings and evenings, and damp, chilly days.

Cruise Check List

Although the needs of your cruise will vary with your individual requirements, following is a basic list of those items that you will probably need. What you take will depend on your taste, your boat, the group accompanying you on the cruise, and the length of time you plan to be out. A careful check of this list will prevent you from waking some dark night when you are at anchor in strange waters and discovering that the flashlight you need so badly is in the bottom drawer of your kitchen cabinet at home.

1. Running lights—red and green, plus a white stern light
2. Life jackets—one for every person aboard, plus buoyant seat cushions
3. Fire extinguisher—at least one
4. First-aid kit and manual
5. Trailer hitch
6. Safety chain
7. Trailer stoplight
8. Boat hook
9. Extra oil
10. Spare fuel tank
11. Top and side curtains
12. Tools, hull repair kit, extra spark plugs

13. Spare motor parts (shear pins, props, and motor manual)
14. Anchor (perhaps two anchors . . . one light and one heavy)
15. Flares in a watertight container, or a flare pistol and cartridges
16. Extra line—about 100 feet
17. Paddle
18. Fenders
19. Bilge pump
20. Flashlight
21. Compass
22. Charts
23. Horn and/or whistle

If you are going on an extended cruise or plan to camp out for several days, the following items should be added to your check list in order to avoid forgetting something in the last-minute rush:

1. Portable radio
2. Tableware
3. Ice cooler
4. Portable stove
5. Pots and pans
6. Can opener
7. Emergency rations
8. Matches
9. Bathing suits
10. Sweaters
11. Raincoats

12. Water skis and tow rope
13. Water purification tablets
14. Sleeping bags or bedding
15. Insect repellent
16. Binoculars
17. Toilet paper
18. Knife
19. Hatchet
20. Soap
21. Towels
22. Camera
23. Twine
24. Fishing tackle
25. Sun glasses
26. Waterproof box for currency and identification cards

CRUISING IN COMPANY

A group cruise calls for the same careful planning, preparation, and organization as does an individual cruise. The first step in going on a group cruise is to elect or appoint a cruisemaster. The cruisemaster should be an experienced outboarder and must have a knack for organizing and leading group activities. He appoints other cruise officers to assist him. These usually include:

- Assistant cruisemaster . . . assists in planning cruises, completing arrangements, launching and leading the cruise.

- Scout . . . travels ahead of the main cruise party and detects water hazards, clears and marks channels, and selects landing spots for the rest of the cruise.
- Courier . . . serves as a messenger and contact man between the cruisemaster and other members of the cruise.
- Tailman . . . follows at the rear of the cruise party in order to assist any boat with mechanical trouble.
- First-aid man . . . carries a complete first-aid kit.

The cruisemaster and his assistants plan thoroughly the entire route of the proposed cruise. They usually travel over the route prior to the cruise in order to locate refueling stations, check and mark danger spots, and check the mileage, time, etc. If it is to be an overnight cruise, the cruisemaster also lines up sleeping accommodations and eating places for the cruise.

The activities and fun you will have aboard your boat are limited only by your imagination. The possibilities are endless. Whether you select to be a "loner" or join up with one of the many boating clubs, you will find that your boat offers a wide range of exciting activities.

GAMES

After you have grown accustomed to your boat and know all the tricks to handling it, you will probably become interested in boating as a group activity. When you get together with your boating club or group of enthusiasts, there are several interesting and exciting ways of enjoying your boat. One of them is a boating gymkhana . . . a test of boating skill by means of games.

The most important thing to remember about playing games with your boat is that the contests require a certain amount of room. Therefore, do not schedule the games in areas where other boats may be passing through, or where swimmers or water skiers are located.

Straight Course Run

In this game, steady, straight steering is emphasized. Set out in a straight line perpendicular to the shore, set pairs of buoys or markers spaced 10 feet apart and with 100 feet between pairs. The contestant embarks properly from beach or pier, starts the engine, runs the course outward, makes a turn and then runs the buoy gauntlet back to the starting point, securing the boat in the approved manner.

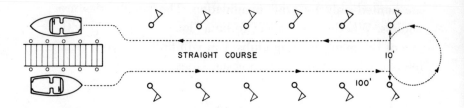

STRAIGHT COURSE   10'   100'

Slalom

Skill in steering, making turns, and controlling speed are the prime emphases in this game. Set buoys or markers out

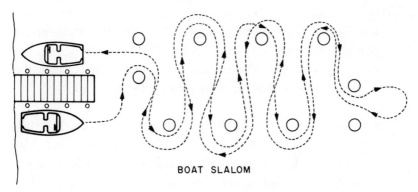

BOAT SLALOM

in pairs so as to form a flat W. Start out from the dock or beach and run through the W, turn and run again in the opposite direction and return to the starting point.

Figure Eight

This familiar ice-skating figure has a place in boating,

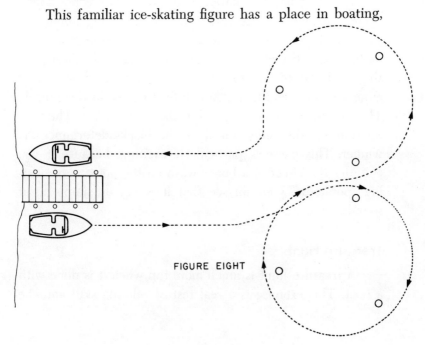

FIGURE EIGHT

too. To develop skill in turning at high speed, set the buoys out to form two adjoining circles. The boatman leaves the dock, runs around the nearer circle clockwise, circles the other counterclockwise, then returns to the dock.

In the three exercises described above, penalties are imposed for hitting buoys, passing them on the wrong side, and for mistakes made in getting underway and in docking. Taking these penalties into consideration, time is the determining factor in the selection of the winner.

The following games are excellent tests of emergency procedures:

Potato Race

Eight brilliantly colored blocks or balls are positioned overboard at even intervals in a line extending about 800 yards offshore. The contestant and his crew get the boat underway, and pick up the block, or "potato," farthest from the beach. He returns to the beach with it and drops it into a box on shore, and then takes off for the next farthest block. The nearest block to the beach is thus left for last. The fastest time for the collection of all the blocks determines the winner. This game is particularly exciting, because if you consider the effect of a boat's wash on the position of floating "potatoes," you can see that it is not as simple as it sounds.

Treasure Hunt

A treasure hunt is much more fun when it is done with a boat. This exercise is a real test of piloting skill and the use of the compass. A multi-legged course is laid out ahead of time on the lake or bay, with each leg ending at a landing where course directions are hidden for the next leg. Contestants are given the course to the first point as they depart. Upon reaching this point, they find the directions for point two, and at point two, they find directions for point three, and so on. Best time around the circuit determines the winner. A suggestion to make things a little more difficult: compass courses may be shown on "clues" in the form of international code flags.

How to Make a Buoy

Buoys can be easily made for these games. Empty one-gallon oil cans with the caps tightly screwed on make good buoys. Paint them white or yellow so they are easy to spot on the water. Fit a mooring line to the handle and anchor the buoy with old sash weights or coffee cans full of rocks or concrete.

CHAPTER EIGHT

Test Your Boating Knowledge

The following set of questions is designed to test your boating knowledge; the answers immediately follow them. Until you understand every question fully and can answer each one correctly, you are not qualified to operate a boat.

Knowing all the answers does not mean you are an expert boatman, but it does indicate you have sufficient knowledge to operate a boat. The true test of a boatman is found in how he skippers his boat in all situations.

The questions and answers are based on the suggested examination for seamanship students of the Outboard Boating Club of America.

1. What are the two basic types of boat hulls?
   Planing and displacement.
2. What are two major causes of boating mishaps?

Test Your Boating Knowledge

Overloading and overpowering.

3. What is the most important factor in selecting a new outboard rig?
Proper matching of boat, motor, and trailer.

4. What equipment is required for a Class 1 motorboat operating on federal waters?
Lifesaving devices for everyone on board, a fire extinguisher, a hand, mouth, or mechanical whistle, bow and stern lights.

5. What additional equipment should be carried that is not required by law?
Paddle, anchor and line, first-aid kit, extra approved gas can, flashlight, tool kit, spare propeller and spark plugs, compass, fenders, extra line, and bilge pump.

6. The capacity of a boat is indicated by the number of seats. True or false?
False.

7. What are the five most common causes of boating accidents?
Overloading, overpowering, going out in bad weather, failure to keep a sharp lookout, high-speed turns.

8. What is the minimum height of the state or Coast Guard boat numbers that must be displayed on both sides of the bow?
Three inches.

9. In backing up, what direction does the trailer turn when you turn the steering wheel of the car to the right?
Left.

10. Why should you avoid sitting on life preservers?
This packs the filler and makes them less buoyant.

11. If the bow of your outboard boat rides high, while the stern digs in, this usually means the motor is tilted too far out or too far in?
    Too far out.

12. When starting a gearshift motor, you should wait until there are no boats around, then cast off lines before starting the engine. True or false?
    False.

13. What are the two rules to remember when starting a non-gearshift outboard motor?
    Remain seated facing forward, and be sure the way ahead is clear.

14. On the waterways, what are the three basic situations in which nautical rules of the road apply?
    Crossing, overtaking, meeting head on.

15. In most cases, the boat on the right has the right of way. True or false?
    True.

16. Under most conditions, motorboats must yield their right of way to rowboats and sailboats. True or false?
    True.

17. What is the area from dead ahead to 2 points aft of your starboard beam called?
    Danger zone.

18. What is the boat that has the right of way called?
    The privileged vessel.

19. What is the boat that yields the right of way called?
    The burdened vessel.

20. When a boat is being overtaken by another boat, which one is the privileged vessel?
    The boat being overtaken.

21. While the burdened vessel is required to slow down, or turn, or take whatever action is necessary to avoid collision, what are the requirements for the privileged vessel?
    The privileged vessel must hold its course and speed until the burdened vessel is clear.
22. What is the first thing to do when a person goes overboard?
    Stop the propeller.
23. What are the steps to take if caught in a storm offshore?
    Slow down, seat passengers in lowest part of the boat, keep bow headed at angle into waves, and head for nearest landing site.
24. What are the three basic types of navigational aids?
    Spar, can, and nun buoys.
25. When proceeding upstream or entering a harbor, should you keep the red buoys on your right or left?
    Right.
26. A horizontally striped buoy indicates what?
    An underwater obstruction.
27. What does one blast of a boat's whistle mean?
    I shall pass you on my port side.
28. What does two blasts on a boat's whistle mean?
    I shall pass you on my starboard side.
29. What does three blasts on a boat's whistle mean?
    I have my engines in reverse.
30. How many times the depth of the water should the anchor line be?
    At least five times.
31. What does a buoy with black and white vertical stripes mean?

The center of the channel.

32. Why must anchor lines have slack in them?
To cushion shock, keep strain on the anchor low, and provide for changes in water level.

33. Do gasoline vapors rise or settle in the bilges?
They settle in the bilges.

34. What does a small-craft storm warning flag look like?
A red triangular pennant.

35. What are three recognized distress signals?
Raising arms to shoulder level and lowering slowly, red flares, constant sounding of horn, whistle, or bell.

36. On rivers, vessels going downstream usually have the right of way over vessels coming upstream. True or false?
True.

37. A boat owner is responsible for any damage caused by his boat's wake. True or false?
True.

38. When dropping anchor, should you lower it slowly, or simply heave it over the side?
Lower it slowly.

39. How should you dislodge an anchor that is fouled?
Circle the anchor, keeping the anchor line taut.

40. What two things should you first check when coming in for a landing at a pier?
Wind and current.

41. What should you do when there is a strong wind blowing toward your docking point?
Stop the propeller a few yards out and drift in.

42. What should you do when there is a strong wind blowing away from your mooring?

242

Come in at a sharp angle until the bow makes contact.

43. When your boat is beached with bow on land and stern in the water, what can you do to prevent it from being washed on shore?

Put out an anchor over the stern.

Glossary of Nautical Terms

Every sport has its own language, and boating is no exception. The language of the sea is probably the most captivating of all because the very sound and meaning of the words bring romance and adventure to mind. Samuel Clemens, author of *The Adventures of Huckleberry Finn,* was so entranced by the sound of the words used on the river that he used a nautical term, Mark Twain, as his pen name.

A broad nautical vocabulary is the sign of an experienced boatman, and if you attain this distinction, you will acquire an extensive vocabulary. Here is a list of commonly used words that will start you off in the right direction. Not all nautical words are included because it would take another book twice the size of this one to list them. Sailing terminology has been excluded, since this book deals only with powerboats.

ABAFT: Used when indicating a direction toward the rear of the boat.

ABEAM: Used when describing the location of an object that is directly on the right or left of your boat. It signifies the position of an object that is at right angles to the keel.

ABOARD: Within or upon a boat.

ABOVE: On land you would say "upstairs." If you're in the cabin, you can use "above" to refer to something or someone on deck.

ADRIFT: Floating at random; moving without direction; at the mercy of wind and current.

AFLOAT: Borne on the water; resting on the surface of the water.

AFOUL: Entangled or snagged in any way.

AFT: At or toward the rear, or pertaining to the rear of a boat.

AGROUND: When the boat rests on the ground as a result of insufficient water to keep it completely afloat.

AMIDSHIPS: In the middle part of the boat; also, midway as to width of the boat.

ANCHOR: A weighted object of varying size and shape, attached to a boat by a line or chain. When dropped overboard, it fastens itself to the bottom and holds the boat in the position desired.

ASTERN: In or at the rear of a boat. When a boat is backing up, it is going astern. An object in back of the boat is astern.

ATHWARTSHIPS: Across the boat from side to side.

BAIL: To dip water out of a boat.

BALLAST: Any material attached to a boat to make it ride deeper in the water.

BARNACLES: A name applied to a type of marine life that adheres to submerged bottoms of boats or rocks. They are especially bothersome in salt water.

BATTENS: Strips of wood used to keep canvas taut.

BEAM: The width of a boat at the maximum point.

BEARING: The position of a boat to an object, or the point of the compass in which an object is seen.

BELAY: To fasten, or make fast, by winding a line around a cleat or belaying pin. Also a command to stop.

BELOW: In a cabin or under the deck, when you are standing on deck.

BERTH: A space occupied by a boat riding or ranging at anchor. Any situation or place where a boat lies, or can lie, whether at anchor or at a dock. A sleeping place or bunk.

BILGE: That part of the bottom of the boat that is most nearly flat. Area beneath the floor boards.

BINNACLE: A case or box in which the compass and a light are kept.

BITTS: A frame of two strong pieces of timber or metal sticking up from the fore part of the boat, on which anchor lines are fixed.

BLOCK: One or more pulleys.

BOAT HOOK: Long pole with a metal hook at one end. It is handy for picking up a mooring or holding the boat off the dock.

BOLLARD: A thick short upright post used to fasten lines.

BOOT TOP: Thin stripe of paint at the water line. It derives its name from *boot topping,* the operation of cleaning a boat's bottom near the surface of the water by scraping off the slime and applying a protective mixture.

BOW: The stem, prow, or front of a boat. The rounding part of a boat's side forward.

BROACH: To incline suddenly to windward. Exposing the hull as to almost upset or capsize.

BROADSIDE: The whole of a boat's side above the water line from bow to stern.

BULKHEAD: A partition that forms a compartment or watertight chamber. A wall on a boat.

BUNK: A bed on a boat.

BUOY: A floating object anchored in a position to indicate channels or dangerous rocks or bars.

BUOYAGE: A series of buoys to indicate a channel or course for boats.

BUTTOCK: The round part of a boat abaft.

CABIN: An enclosed houselike structure on a boat.

CAPSIZE: To upset or overturn a boat.

CAST OFF: To let go the lines and get underway.

CAULK: To drive tarred or other material into seams of a hull to prevent their admitting water.

CHANNEL: The deeper part of a body of water where the current flows, or which is most convenient for the course of a boat. Can be marked by buoys.

CHART: A marine map showing some part of the earth's surface with coasts, islands, rocks, banks, channels, or entrances to harbors. Used to regulate the boat's course.

CHOCK: A metal fitting, having two short horn-shaped projections curving inward, between which lines are passed during docking or anchoring.

CHOP: A term used to describe short waves caused by wind and tide or current.

CLEATS: A fitting of wood or metal on a boat, used to secure lines.

COAMING: Sides of open areas above deck to keep water from running into the boat.

COCKPIT: An open area with seats where passengers or the skipper sits.

COMMISSIONING: The act of preparing and launching your boat. Also, removing a boat from the water and preparing it for winter.

COMPANIONWAY: A stairway leading from the deck to the cabin. A passageway on a boat.

COMPASS: An instrument used for directing or ascertaining the course of a boat.

CUDDY: A locker or cupboard on a boat.

CURRENT: Water moving continuously in one direction.

CUTWATER: The fore part of a boat's hull that cuts the water.

DECK: A horizontal platform or floor extending from side to side of a boat.

DINGHY: A small boat used to service a larger boat.

DOCK: A place artificially formed along the water's edge to receive boats. It can be floating or permanently built into the ground.

DRAFT: A perpendicular depth of the hull from the water line to the lowest point of the boat.

DRAMAMINE: A drug used to combat seasickness.

DRY ROT: A rapid decay of timber due to fungi. It usually results from lack of proper ventilation.

EDDY: A small circular movement of water.

ELECTROLYSIS: The process of chemical decomposition of hull fittings by electric current passing through salt water.

FAST: When around boats, you don't tie things, you make them fast.

FASTENINGS: In boat construction, all screws, nails, rivets, and bolts.

FENDER: Variously shaped objects made from plastic, rubber, rope, or canvas, used alongside the boat to keep it from becoming scratched or gouged.

FITTINGS: All hardware attached to a boat.

FORE: Toward the front of the boat; forward.

FRAMES: The ribs of a hull. In wooden boats, the planks are attached to the frames.

FREEBOARD: The portion of the boat between the rail or gunwale and the water line.

GALLEY: An area where cooking is done on board.

GAM: A herd of whales. A friendly conversation between crews.

GEAR: A term applied to all equipment and rigging on a boat.

GUNWALE, GUNNEL: The upper edge of a boat's side; the rail.

HATCH: An opening in a deck, floor or roof, affording passage for persons or goods.

HEAD: The boat's toilet.

HEAVE: To throw. You "heave" a line.

HELM: The instrument by which a boat is steered, consisting of a rudder, tiller, wheel, etc. Specifically, a bar which turns the rudder.

HELMSMAN: One who operates the helm. The skipper.

HOLD: That portion of the boat's interior below the deck.

HOOK: A nautical term for the anchor.

HULL: The body of a boat, exclusive of cabin and objects above the gunwale.

INBOARD: All that's inside the boat. An engine that is permanently installed within the hull is an inboard engine.

INBOARD-OUTBOARD: A term applied to boats which have an inboard engine mounted near the transom, and hooked to an outdrive similar to that of an outboard engine.

KEEL: The timber running down the center of the boat at the lowest point.

KNOT: A nautical mile equal to 6,080.27 feet. A land mile has 5,280 feet.

LANDFALL: The first land sighted after a voyage.

LAUNCH: The sliding or moving of a boat from land into water. Also a term applied to a boat that carries the crew to their anchored boat.

LEEWARD: The direction toward which the wind blows. The opposite of windward.

LEEWAY: The leeward drift of a boat.

LIMBER HOLES: Holes in a boat's hull timbers that permit water to run to the lowest point of the hull.

LINE: A nautical term meaning rope.

LIST: A term used when a boat is inclined in one direction; off its normal floating axis.

LOCK: A part of a dam constructed so as to permit passage of boats.

LOCKING THROUGH: The process of moving the boat from one level of water to another through a lock.

LOGBOOK: A book the skipper uses to record all the boat's activities, such as distance traveled, speed, ports, and fuel consumed.

MARINA: A docking area for boats that supplies most of the needs of a boatman.

MARK TWAIN: A term used by nineteenth-century riverboat men when checking the depth of the channel.

MOOR: To confine or secure a boat by lines or anchor.

MOORING: The act of securing a boat to a particular place by means of an anchor or lines. Also, that which moors or secures a boat.

N.A.E.B.M.: National Association of Engine and Boat Manufacturers.

NAVIGABLE: A term applied to waterways that permit the movement of a boat without striking sunken or hidden objects.

OAR: A long piece of timber, flat at one end and round at the other, used to propel a boat.

OBC: Outboard Boating Club of America.

OUTBOARD: A term applied to a motor that can be removed or attached to the transom. Also, any object outside the hull.

PAINTER: A line that is used to pull or make fast a small boat or dinghy.

PIER: A structure built on the edge of the water to accommodate boats.

PORT: Looking forward or toward the front of the boat, port is the left side.

PORTHOLES: Holes or circular windows in the side of a boat.

QUARTER: The aft side of a boat.

RAIL: The side of a boat above the deck.

RIGGING: A term applied to all the lines on a boat.

ROW: To propel a boat by means of oars.

RUDDER: A flat object protruding from the stern that directs the boat's course. The rudder is moved by the tiller or wheel.

SCOPE: The length of the anchor line that is actually in use.

SEA ANCHOR: A bucket or canvas bag thrown overboard with a line attached to the boat. It reduces the movement of the boat.

SEAM: The space between two planks. Caulking is applied to a seam to make it watertight.

SEASICKNESS: The sickness or nausea caused by the motion of a boat.

SEXTANT: A nautical instrument for measuring the altitudes of celestial objects and their apparent angular distances, thereby determining the latitude and longitude at sea. It gives you the boat's location when out of sight of landmarks.

SHEER: The longitudinal curve or bend of a boat's deck or sides.

SHOAL: A sand bar or hill near the surface of the water. Also, a shallow place in a lake, river, pond, or sea.

SKEG: The lowermost part of an outboard engine.

SOUND: The action of determining the depth of the water.

STAFF: An upright pole with a light or flag on it.

STARBOARD: Looking toward the bow, it's the right side of the boat.

STEM: An upright curved piece of timber to which the sides of the boat are attached at the fore end.

STERN: The back end of a boat; the aft part.

STORM WARNINGS: Signals indicating the weather conditions of offshore waters.

STRAKE: Continuous line of planking on a boat's side, from stem to stern.

SUPERSTRUCTURE: All the construction extending above the deck level of a boat.

SWELL: Actually a large wave without a crest which gives the impression that the sea is undulating. It is usually caused by a distant storm or disturbance.

TIDAL WAVE: The wave caused by the union of two waves, one produced by the attraction to the sun, the other by that of the moon.

TIDE: The alternate rising and falling of the waters of the ocean, including connecting bays, rivers, etc. The action is caused by the gravitational influence of the sun and moon, primarily the moon.

TOPSIDES: All of the boat above the water line. Also, the deck is referred to as topsides.

TRANSOM: In outboard boats, it's the flat aft part of the boat where the outboard motor is attached. In inboard boats, it's the flat aft part of the boat.

TRIM: The position of a boat in the water as a result of the load placed in the boat.

TROLLING: Fishing from a slow-moving boat.

U.S.C.G.: United States Coast Guard.

U.S.C.G.A.: United States Coast Guard Auxiliary.

USPS: United States Power Squadrons.

UNDERWAY: A boat is said to be underway when it is moving through the water.

WAKE: The track left by a boat in the water, formed by the meeting of the water which rushed from each side to fill the space which the boat makes in passing through it. Also, all waves caused by a boat.

WATER LINE: A horizontal line supposed to be described by the surface of the water on the sides of the boat. Also, any line on the side indicating depth of the hull in the water.

WHARF: A construction on the edge of the water where boats load and unload.

WHEEL: Any construction used for steering a boat. It is connected to the rudder or tiller or motor. The propeller of an outboard engine is often called the wheel.

WINDWARD: The direction from which the wind is blowing. Toward the wind.

YAW: To swerve or roll from side to side.

Suggested Additional Reading

Allen, Jim J. *Boating: A Beginning Guide.* Ronald Press, New York, 1958.

Anderson, Edwin P. *Audels Outboard Motor and Boating Guide.* Audels.

Aymar, Brandt, and Marshall, John. *Guide to Boatmanship, Seamanship, and Safe Boat Handling.* Chilton, New York, 1960.

Canfield, James D. *Fitting Out and Repairing Your Boat.* Chilton, New York, 1960.

Chapman, Charles R. *Cruising Boats with Your Budget.* Harper, New York.

Suggested Additional Reading

——. *Seamanship: A Practical Manual.* Motor Boating. New York, 1960.

——. *Piloting, Seamanship and Small Boat Handling.* Motor Boating, New York.

Drake, Lauren and Madge. *Getting the Most out of a Power Boat.* Norton, New York, 1963.

How to Build 35 Modern Motor Boats. Motor Boating, New York.

Hutinson, James. *All About Boats.* Popular Mechanics Press, Chicago, 1958.

*Janes, Edward C. *A Boy and His Boat.* Mcrae Smith, Philadelphia, 1963.

*Klein, David. *Beginning with Boats.* Crowell, New York, 1962.

——. *Your Outboard Cruiser.* Norton, New York, 1954.

Lane, Carl Daniel. *New Boatman's Manual.* Norton, New York, 1962.

*Liebers, Arthur. *Complete Book of Water Sports.* Coward, New York, 1962.

———. *Motor Boat Owner's Handbook.* Ottenheimer, New York.

*Lydgate, Constance and William. *Power and Sail.* Macmillan, New York, 1963.

Modern Motor Boat Plans and Designs. Motor Boating, New York.

*Parsons, Tom. *Boys' Book of Outboard Boating.* Macmillan, New York, 1959.

*Pearsall, Bill. *Young Sportsman's Guide to Motorboating.* Nelson, New York, 1962.

Scharff, Robert. *Complete Boating Handbook.* McGraw, New York, 1955.

———. *Complete Book of Outboard Cruising.* Putnam, New York, 1960.

True, Frank C. *Small Boat Owner's Guide.* Lantern, New York, 1956.

Vark, Ernest. *Complete Outboard Boating Manual.* American Technical Society, Chicago, 1958.

Walliser, Blair. *Basic Seamanship and Safe Boat Han-

dling. Doubleday, New York, 1962.

Whittier, Bob. *Guide to Equipping Your Boat.* Chilton, New York, 1959.

* *Of special interest to young people.*